BUNKER HILL

PETER REESE DOYLE

DRUMS
of WAR

Providence
Foundation

Bunker Hill

Published by:
The Providence Foundation
P.O. Box 6759
Charlottesville, VA 22906
(804) 978-4535
provfdn@aol.com
www.providencefoundation.com

Cover illustration:
Corky Nell

The Providence Foundation is a Christian educational organization whose purpose is to assist in the development of liberty, justice, and prosperity among the nations by teaching and equipping people in a Biblical philosophy of life. The Foundation teaches Christian principles of government and politics, economics and business, arts and sciences, education and family life, using historical models which illustrate their application.

Printed in the United States of America

ISBN 1-887456-08-2

Bunker Hill

Peter Reese Doyle

TABLE OF CONTENTS

WITH THANKS TO GOD

for

THE UNIVERSITY

OF

WASHINGTON AND LEE

for
Honorable Comrades
Inspiring Teachers
and
Two Great Men

FRANK J. GILLIAM

Dean of Students

JAMES GRAHAM LEYBURN

Dean of the University

MASSACHUSETTS
April - June, 1775

In Massachusetts British Troops marched on to Lexington,
To seize the Patriot Leaders, and wreck their Stores and
  Guns;
But Paul Revere rode desperately to warn the Towns and
  Farms,
And soon the Night was shattered by the Sound of the
  Alarms

That rang from Churchbells, Town to Town, and through
  the Countryside,
And woke the sleeping Citizens and brought Men side by
  side
In marching ranks to Lexington, where they saw the Slain
The Patriots the British Troops shot on their Village Green.

Militiamen from other Towns formed Ranks and hurried
  round,
They struck the dreaded Redcoats as they left the Blood-
  stained Ground,
They shot them as they fled the fatefield of Lexington,
They drove them back to Boston and the shelter of its Guns.

And then the Patriots formed a Guard round Boston and its
  Bay,
And bottled up the Tyrants in the Town wherein they lay.
But when the British Troops attacked – to break our Peo-
  ples' Will –
They lost a Thousand Redcoats on the Slopes 'round Bun-
  ker Hill.

The time is now at hand which must probably determine whether Americans are to be freemen or slaves; whether they are to have any property they can call their own; whether their houses and farms are to be pillaged and destroyed, and themselves consigned to a state of wretchedness from which no human efforts will deliver them. The fate of unborn millions will now depend on God, on the courage and conduct of this army. Our cruel and unrelenting enemy leaves us only the choice of brave resistance, or the most abject submission. We have, therefore, to resolve to conquer or die.

**General George Washington
Address to the Continental Army, 1776**

☆ **Chapter One** ☆

Virginia Arms for War

Andrew Hendricks and Nathan Edwards raced their horses down the street, whooping wildly as they rode. Clouds of dust rose from the flashing hooves of their galloping steeds, sparks flew up when the iron horseshoes struck rocks in the road, and a flock of chickens scattered squawking in fright before them. Arriving at their homes, Nathan pulled up first, leaped from the saddle, tied his mount hastily to the rail and dashed up the steps and into his house.

Andrew hauled his mount to a stop at the very next home. He too vaulted from the saddle, threw his reins over the tie rail, and ran toward the steps. Leaping these with a single bound he burst through the door — and ran right into Nathan's sister Sarah.

"Ohhh!" Sarah cried out as she fell back against the paneled wall, her blue eyes wide with shock and surprise.

"Andrew!" his sister Rachel exclaimed, backing hastily out of the way.

"Sorry!" Andrew mumbled, face red as he helped Sarah steady herself. Then he forgot Sarah. "Rachel, where's father?"

"Right here!" William Hendricks replied, walking quickly out of the kitchen and followed closely by Nelson Edwards, the father of Sarah and Nathan.

"What do you mean by running into Sarah like that?" Hendricks asked his son, his tanned face showing great surprise. A tall, lean man, with dark hair and penetrating dark eyes, he waited for Andrew's reply.

"Forgive me, father..." Andrew began, but his father cut him short.

"It's Sarah who must forgive you, Andrew."

"Yes, sir," he said, gulping. "I'm sorry, Sarah," he said, thoroughly embarrassed now. "I didn't mean to run into you."

Sarah smiled her forgiveness — but Andrew, greatly excited by the message he bore, had already turned his head back to his father and Mr. Edwards. "Mr. Randolph's back from the Congress in Philadelphia!" he blurted.

"What?" William Hendricks said, glancing quickly at Nelson Edwards. "Already?"

"Yes sir," Andrew said. "And the volunteer company escorted him back into town! Nathan and I did too! We rode with the mounted men! It was like a victory parade!"

Just then the door burst open and Nathan Edwards ran in. He crashed straight into his sister, Sarah, knocking her roughly into Andrew. Andrew stumbled back into the wall, reaching his arms around Sarah's waist to keep her from falling.

"Hold on!" Nelson Edwards cried out, staring sternly at his son. "What's going on, Nathan?"

"I'm sorry, father!" Nathan said quickly. "Sorry, Sarah," he added.

Sarah wasn't really hurt, but her face was flushed again with confusion. She didn't know whether she should be mad at her brother for knocking into her – or embarrassed that Andrew was still holding her fast in his strong arms.

But Nathan had forgotten her already. "Did you tell them the news?" he asked Andrew breathlessly. Andrew seemed to forget Sarah also — although he still held her firmly — and opened his mouth to reply. But Nathan was so excited that he couldn't wait.

"Things are happening fast, Father!" Nathan said. "Andrew and I were just riding into town..."

Now Andrew could contain himself no longer. Forgetting that he still held his arms around Sarah, he interrupted Nathan, his brown eyes wide with excitement. "We'd just ridden back into town, and were passing Tim Collins' house, when he galloped out of his yard yelling something about Mr. Randolph's return. So we turned around and galloped after him."

"It was grand, Father," Nathan broke in, waving a long arm, hazel eyes shining with excitement. "Mr. Randolph was the president of the whole Continental Congress when it met in Philadelphia! And he came back for the Virginia Assembly meeting. And our men — with rifles and muskets! — rode beside him, while others marched in front and behind, just like a military escort! They're calling him the 'father' of our country, now. And Andrew and I were riding right with them!"

William Hendricks and Nelson Edwards exchanged grins at their sons' excitement. Edwards glanced quickly at his daughter, Sarah. "Are you all right after these wild men crashed into you?"

"Yes, Father," she smiled, blue eyes laughing at the overpowering excitement that gripped the two boys. Her almostblack hair fell to the shoulders of her long blue dress. She'd recovered her breath, but was now blushing furiously, because Andrew, in his excitement, had forgotten to let her go! His face, like Nathan's, shone with high excitement at the thought of the military cavalcade in which he and Nathan had just participated.

"Then maybe you could let Sarah go, Andrew," Mr. Hendricks said to his son, trying to keep a broad grin off his face at Andrew's instant confusion. He couldn't resist adding: "She seems to be all right now, and could probably stand up all by herself — if you'd just let her!"

"Yes, sir!" Andrew said hastily, appalled with embarrassment that he'd forgotten to let her go. He released her so quickly that she stumbled again and lost her balance. Her father reached out quickly and steadied her, unable to keep from laughing at the pair's confusion. It was impossible to tell whose face was more crimson now, Sarah's, or Andrew's.

"Sorry, Sarah," Andrew mumbled, unable to look at her, and wishing he could fall through the floor. Nathan laughed out loud.

Just then Mrs. Hendricks came out of the kitchen. Andrew's mother was tall, with long reddish-brown hair and twinkling gray eyes. "Bring them back here, William. We'll give the boys some cold cider. Maybe that will cool them down," she laughed, looking at Andrew pointedly. His face became even more crimson.

They all trooped back into the kitchen. "Sit down, boys," William Hendricks said, as he and Nelson Edwards took their chairs and picked up the mugs from which they'd been drinking when the boys had first rushed into the house.

"Help me pour, Girls," Mrs. Hendricks said, reaching for a large pitcher of cider. Sarah and Rachel took two mugs from the shelf above the sideboard and let Mrs. Hendricks fill these. Then they took these over to the boys. Sarah's face was still red with embarrassment, and as she handed Andrew a mug she kept her eyes down and didn't look at him.

"Thanks," he mumbled, taking the mug with nervous hands. He avoided her eyes too, and took a deep drink from the cool cider. Then he took another.

Sarah and Rachel then sat down with their own mugs of cider, eager to hear what their brothers had to say. Rachel was trying not to laugh at her brother's and Sarah's embarrassment. But she couldn't help grinning at Sarah — until Sarah kicked her shin.

"My goodness!" Mrs. Hendricks exclaimed, as she saw the boys drink down the cider. "I'd better pour you more!" She brought over the pitcher and filled their mugs again.

Thanking her hastily, Andrew and Nathan turned once more to their fathers, and began to tell what they'd learned from the crowd of men around Mr. Randolph. Their eyes flashed with excitement as they described the marching and riding escort for Mr. Peyton Randolph. Then they began to tell of the Congress in Philadelphia.

"Mr. Randolph said that the colonies are standing fast, and standing together," Andrew said, obviously proud of the unity displayed by the delegates to the Continental Congress. "They're not going to let the British Government deal with — and conquer — them one at a time."

The older men looked at each other quickly, clearly pleased to hear this. William Hendricks spoke first. "Well, Mr. Randolph confirms what our Virginia House of Burgesses has already decided: the colonies **must** stand together! We cannot allow Great Britain to treat with us separately, or they'd just enslave us one at a time! That's very encouraging," he concluded quietly.

"It is," Nelson Edwards agreed. "We'll either stand together, or we'll hang separately, as Benjamin Franklin said. He's right, too. If the British can make separate agreements with each colony, they'll just eat us up one after the other — beginning with Massachusetts, where they've got their army and navy." He sighed and took out his pipe. "Imagine! The British Parliament, with the King's approval, suspended the Charter of the Massachusetts Colony! That's the Colony's constitution! And that means that there's no law for the Colony except what the British Parliament **says** is law — on any given day! This destroys the foundation of liberty, and puts the citizens of Massachusetts under the tyranny of men in government who have no limits to their power! And the British will do that to every other Colony, one at a time."

"If we let them," William Hendricks said quietly.

"If we let them," Nelson Edwards agreed. "But who would have thought that the constitutional liberties the American Colonies have enjoyed for over a hundred and fifty years would be wiped out by government action like this?" he asked, shaking his head.

"They won't, not if the Colonies stand fast, and stand together," William Hendricks replied.

"That's what they're doing, sir," Andrew said. "Capt. Innes asked you and Mr. Nelson to come to the Raleigh Tavern tonight. The volunteer company will be there, and some other gentlemen. Mr. Randolph wants to tell the news from the Constitutional Congress."

The two men glanced at each other. "We'll get the latest information," Edwards said. "Maybe that will help us sort through all these rumors we've been hearing."

"I wonder if it will," Carolyn Hendricks asked quietly. She came and sat in the chair beside her husband, her usually smiling face very serious, her gray eyes troubled. "For weeks now, Williamsburg's been swept with rumors of every kind. Each ship that lands in the nearby rivers brings mail with the wildest stories and alarms. Each piece of news we hear seems more threatening than the last. You know the desperate tales the newspapers have published, William. How can we know what is true and what is not? What can we believe of all the things we hear?"

"Not a lot, Carolyn, not a lot," her husband agreed. "That's why it's best to wait before believing what people say is 'news'! Most of what folks call 'news' is nothing but rumor — when it's not lies and slander. All the more reason for us to go to that meeting tonight and learn what may be the truth about the Congress." His lean tanned face broke into a grin as he looked around the table at his family and friends, dark eyes shining: "Imagine! A Congress with delegations from almost all of the colonies! Who would have thought it possible?"

"It would not have been possible," Nelson Edwards said quietly, "if the British government had not made so many stupid mistakes."

"That's true, isn't it," Carolyn Hendricks observed thoughtfully. "Few people in the colonies even thought about separating from Great Britain. We certainly never thought of waging war against her!"

"But why is all this happening, Father?" Rachel asked.

"Rachel," William Hendricks replied, setting down his mug, "the merchant and financial leaders of Great Britain see the American Colonies as their greatest market, the best place for them to send their goods and make their profits. They forbid us to manufacture many products, forcing us to buy them from England at very high prices. These merchants put their friends in places of power when they can, so that their government will make laws to promote their own businesses. This happens in every nation, all through history. We Americans have been protesting these new tyrannous laws for a number of years. We've even boycotted their goods, and this has hurt English business. So the King and his cabinet officers intend to subjugate us entirely to prevent us from stopping England's policies against us. They're bent on enslaving us for the benefit of those businessmen the King favors."

"But the King is supposed to be head over the colonies, isn't he?" Sarah asked. "And doesn't he rule through each colony's own Charter and Governor and Legislature?"

"He's supposed to," her father said. "But King George is in alliance with England's financial and manufacturing leaders, and he needs their support for his wars and policies. Those men see us only as a market for their goods, and a supplier of the raw materials they need. They use England's government — Parliament — to promote their businesses. So the King's joined with some of them and declared us enemies for resisting Parliament's new laws. And those new laws make claims to rule us totally."

"Then the King has broken his constitutional responsibility to protect our liberties and laws," Carolyn Hendricks said.

"That's right, Carolyn," her husband replied soberly. "He's letting the Parliament of Great Britain assume total and supreme power over the colonies — 'in all things whatsoever'! Those are the very words in their recent law. They claim to rule us in every area of life — they've declared us slaves, in effect. Three million people in North America are now ruled by a handful of men in London — some of whom are very wicked personally! We have no legal protection, because law is what those men in government say it is."

"That's what so frightening to those who don't belong to the Church of England," Nelson Edwards added, "especially in the Northern and Middle Colonies. Many of those colonies were established specifically by Protestants who wanted their religion and their society to be ruled by the Bible, not by English Bishops. That's why their forefathers left England. Every one of their Charters has the Bible as the basis for its laws. But English Bishops want to make the Church of England — the Anglican Church — the only official Church for all the colonies, just as it is in England."

"If that happened," William Hendricks added soberly, "every American citizen would have to pay to support that church. Last year, in fact, Parliament made Roman Catholicism the official religion of Canada — just by governmental edict! This shows their total power over even the religion in North America! If they did that in the American Colonies, the congregations would no longer have the right to choose their own pastors, or demand sermons from the Bible. The Protestant Colonies would see an end to their religious freedoms. Those Northern and Middle Colonies especially see this as a matter of religious survival — more than many of us in Virginia realize."

"But the English Church in Virginia still makes it hard on Presbyterians and Baptists, doesn't it Father?" Sarah asked. "Remember the preachers they jailed just recently, just because they weren't ordained in the Church of England. And our Presbyterian preachers have always had trouble from the magistrates in Virginia."

"You're right, Sarah. The Church of England men in Virginia have persecuted the Presbyterians and the Baptists. That's another injustice that Patrick Henry has been trying to stop. Thousands of Presbyterians have come into Virginia from Scotland in recent years, and thousands of Baptists as well. These people remember the persecutions and tortures they and their forefathers endured in England and Ireland and Scotland, first from the Church of Rome, and then from the Church of England. They know what can happen to them and to their children if Parliament can do anything it wants regarding their religion."

"So there are other fundamental reasons why the colonies sent delegates to that Convention in Philadelphia," Nelson Edwards said, glancing around the room. He particularly wanted the children to understand this. "If we let those men in London get away with their recent claim to be our absolute masters, in government as well as in religion, unchecked by constitution and law, we'll lose all the rights of free Englishmen which our forefathers came to this New World to secure."

"We'll probably have to fight!" William Hendricks said quietly, looking soberly at his friend. "We owe it to our children. We've got to fight to preserve for them the freedoms our fathers gave to us."

Then Hendricks decided to change the subject. Standing quickly, he turned to his son. "Andrew, you'd better unsaddle the mare and dry her off."

"Yes, sir," Andrew replied. "Thanks for the cider, Mother," he said, smiling as he rose.

"I'll do the same," Nathan said. "We rode hard getting back here with the news. Thank you, Mrs. Hendricks."

"You're welcome always, Nathan," she smiled.

"May we go with them, mother?" Rachel asked quickly, as the boys rose to leave.

"Certainly, Rachel, but don't forget that you two are helping me and your mother bake today."

"Yes, ma'am," Rachel replied, as she and Sarah rose hastily and went after their brothers. Sarah's cheeks were still quite red, but she appeared to have regained her composure.

Nelson Edwards rose also. "Thank you, Carolyn," he smiled. "I'll go tell Mary what we've learned."

Hendricks followed his friend from the room, through the hall, and out onto the front porch. "I'll be particularly interested to learn if Mr. Randolph thinks it's still safe for our schooner to sail to New York," he said quietly. "We won't let it sail if the British are threatening our shipping."

"That we will not!" Nelson Edwards agreed. "But we've heard nothing yet to make us think the coastal trade is in danger of British raids. Not yet, at least."

The two men stood silently in thought, looking out at the street. Andrew was leading his horse by the reins, while he waved his other hand animatedly, describing to Sarah and Rachel his and Nathan's ride with the volunteer company. The girls were laughing at something he'd said, and the two watching fathers smiled at the obvious excitement and enjoyment of the youngsters.

Glancing to their left, they saw that Nathan had jumped on his mount and was riding to the barn behind his home. Across the street, a mother was working in the vegetable garden beside her house, and her young children were helping her. Two Negroes walked by the Hendrick's house carrying baskets of vegetables, laughing as they talked.

Nothing could have looked more serene, the two men were thinking. But nothing could have been more deceptive. War was brewing. Many people in the American Colonies knew that its coming was inevitable if the colonists were to preserve their political and religious liberties. Yet many others didn't believe this; they still hoped that a way would be found to persuade the British to revoke their plans to send armies and navies to subdue North America.

"The schooner's all ready," William Hendricks said finally, breaking the silence. "Loaded to the gunwales, in fact. We'll make a lot of money with this shipment to New York, Nelson."

"That we will," his friend replied. "Our schooner — and our sons — should be safe enough. John Turnbull knows what to do if there's any sign of danger. He'll run the boat to shore and leave it there: let the British take our cargo — but not our men!"

"We'll learn more tonight at the meeting in the Raleigh Tavern," Hendricks said as he puffed his long pipe. "Then we can make a final decision."

Chapter Two

"YOU'LL SAIL TO NEWPORT"

Early the next morning, Nathan rushed over to the Hendrick's back porch, leaped the steps, and rushed into the kitchen. "Father and Mother and Sarah are coming," he said to Mrs. Hendricks, who was just taking a tray of muffins from the fireplace.

"Fine, Nathan," she replied with a smile. "How about tasting one of these muffins to see if I cooked them right."

"Yes, ma'am," the tall young man replied, following her to the kitchen table. She took one of the steaming muffins and handed it to him. Just then, Andrew and Rachel came into the kitchen. "Set out some plates, Rachel." her mother said. "And the water's hot — let's make the chocolate."

"Yes, ma'am," Rachel replied, smiling at Nathan as he wolfed down the muffin. "Goodness, Mother, he hasn't eaten for a week! Look — that muffin's gone already!"

"Give him another one, then," her mother said. She set the muffins on a large platter and began to get out the mugs. "You know how hungry boys get when they smell food cooking!" Nodding agreement, Andrew helped himself to another hot muffin.

Nelson and Mary Edwards entered the kitchen, followed by their daughter Sarah. William Hendricks came in after them. The faces of the adults were serious. Only Andrew and Nathan seemed excited as they all sat down around the long table. The younger children were playing in the front room, watched by Andrew's older sister Laura.

"Well, we're sending you boys on the schooner to Newport," William Hendricks said, looking at Andrew and Nathan in turn.

"Mr. Randolph assured us last night that our shipping is still safe, so we're going ahead with this voyage."

"There's really no danger just as long as you don't try to go into Boston Harbor," Nelson Edwards added. "And John Turnbull knows not to go near there."

Mary Edwards spoke then. "And you men are sure that there is no likelihood of a British ship stopping the schooner and kidnapping our sons and the crew for their navy?"

"We're sure, Mary," William Hendricks replied. "Our schooner's a small vessel. It's the bigger ships the British warships stop, those that sail the high seas, with their larger crews who've got men trained for handling the sails of vessels that size. Also, Peyton Randolph told us last night that the British are taking great care not to anger the other colonies — other than Massachusetts, that is. England's not ready for war, not yet — their armies and fleets are scattered around the globe, and they'll need time to assemble them. This situation may not last, but while it does, our small coastal ships are quite safe."

"But why do the British take men from our ships, Father?" Rachel asked. Rachel had brown eyes and light brown hair which fell beside her face in long curls, and her face showed the puzzlement all Americans shared regarding this practice of the British Navy.

"Their warships are all short-handed, Rachel," her father replied. "Their government won't pay enough money to hire the crews they need to man their ships, so they just kidnap Englishmen from the streets of their cities, as well as steal men from American merchant ships. They send gangs of sailors and marines through their port cities back in England to capture any loose men that they can. Then they haul them back to their ships, swear them in as sailors of the King, and keep them prisoner on those ships until they're killed, or are crippled with wounds, or are sick and unable to serve. It's a brutal, a vicious system."

"They've put lots of Methodist preachers in the navy that way," Nelson Edwards added. "That's one way the English State Church has urged the government to end the evangelical movement in England. They'd do the same here if they could!"

"That's horrible!" Sarah said, blue eyes wide with the enormity of arresting honest citizens and making them prisoners of their own country's navy.

"It is indeed, Sarah," William Hendricks said somberly. "But their Navy claims it's the only way they can find enough men to man their warships. That's why American ships have to be so careful when they sail, and do all they can to avoid British warships."

"Well," Nelson Edwards said, leaning forward and taking another muffin from the platter before him, "we wouldn't be sending the schooner up to New York if we thought it might run into danger, especially with you boys on board. We're confident that you'll be safe enough. What we want you to do is accompany the cargo to our agent there, and find out all you can about the possibility of our sending more shipments to New York and Philadelphia."

"Also," he added, "we want to know what arrangements they've made for our shipments to reach them by land, if the British do close our coast to shipping. Our suggestions for doing this as far as Philadelphia are included in the letters you boys will take to Horatio Brown in New York. We want to hear his plans for transporting our products farther north from that city, as well as from Philadelphia."

"We're giving you a lot of responsibility," William Hendricks said, looking soberly at the two boys. "But you both know how to handle that." His lean face broke into a slow smile. Both fathers were immensely proud of their older sons, and the ways in which the two boys accepted the many responsibilities given to them.

"What time do they leave, father?" Sarah asked. She looked somberly at Andrew and Nathan, eyes troubled at the thought of the boys sailing toward the British warships that prowled the waters of the northern colonies.

"They'll leave in an hour, Sarah," Nelson Edwards replied. "John Turnbull's ready to sail."

"Who will bring back their horses, William?" Carolyn Hendricks asked.

"Nelson and I will ride with them to the landing. We'll bring the horses back." He looked at his wife's solemn face. Both mothers, of course, were worried at the prospect of their sons sailing into the waters of the northern colonies. No amount of reassurance could change that, William knew. He glanced over at Nelson Edwards: his friend was thinking the same thing.

"We've put up some food for their journey," Carolyn Hendricks added, pointing to two large baskets beside the door. "This should be enough fresh food for several days, along with the supplies John Turnbull already has on board."

"He said he'd be grateful for the pies Sarah and Rachel offered to make, however," Mary said, "so we put these in the baskets as well."

Andrew and Nathan grinned appreciatively at their sisters, but Sarah and Rachel were so concerned about the possible dangers the boys might face on their journey that neither of them smiled back.

William Hendricks counted out some coins, put these into two small leather wallets, and handed these to his son. "This should be enough, with some to spare, Andrew," he said. "Keep these in different places, so if one is lost or stolen you'll have the other."

Andrew nodded and pocketed the wallets. Nathan's father had already given him his money before they'd left their house.

"And here are letters to Horatio Brown and his partner," William Hendricks continued. "Ask him for a written reply. Learn all you can about his arrangements for transporting goods by land if the British Navy blockades our coasts. Tell him our people in Virginia are collecting more wagons and animals, and that we mean to keep trade going between the colonies, no matter what the British do at sea!"

"Yes, sir," Andrew replied, taking the letters and putting them into the large pocket of his hunting shirt.

Carolyn Hendricks looked across the table at her son. Andrew was almost as tall as his father, and his shoulders were almost as broad. His lean face was pleasant, his brown eyes friendly. But he had an air of quiet competence about him that gave her courage. Yet, she couldn't help being worried. She had a feeling that he was going into danger. She knew that her husband had considered everything about this voyage, and would not consciously send his son where he thought there'd be trouble. But she just couldn't shake the feeling that the boys were going toward harm.

Andrew glanced at his mother and smiled — he always seemed to know when his mother was worried. She saw his thoughtful gaze, and realized that he understood her fears. A slow smile transformed the troubled expression on her face.

William Hendricks rose, went to the cabinet, and returned to the table with the big family Bible. He sat down and opened the book. "I'll read from the eighth chapter of Romans." As he began to read, the two families bent their minds to the great truths of God's absolute sovereign control over all that He had made — including His people. Including Andrew and Nathan. When he finished the chapter, Hendricks led them all in prayer.

CHAPTER THREE

"FIND THE ARMY!"

The schooner was heeled well over, its sails full and taut as the strong breeze drove the sleek and heavily laden craft through the mouth of the York River. John Turnbull held the wheel. His crewman, a free Negro named Thomas, was at the bow, scouting for logs in the river. Just one of these floating trees could wreck a small vessel in a hurry. Andrew and Nathan were midships, coiling lines. They'd sailed with Turnbull often, and knew how to do their part in handling the vessel.

The *Morning Star* was gray, with white trim, displaced over twelve tons, and sailed well in the strong wind. Birds screamed overhead, excited at the boiling wake behind the craft, searching for scraps of food thrown from the boat. Low clouds swept past overhead, but these were unable to conceal the bright sun for long. Small vessels filled the river's mouth, both going and coming. Ahead of the *Morning Star, a* number of tall-masted ships were sailing into the harbor.

"What's that?" Andrew called to John Turnbull, pointing to a sleek warship flying the British flag.

Turnbull, hands on the wheel, looked over at the ship, and squinted in the bright sunlight that sparkled from the waves. Then he called back: "*H. M. S. Magdelen,*" he replied. "That's the ship whose marines stole our powder from the Magazine back in April. That other warship anchored to its left is the *Fowey.*"

Andrew and Nathan gazed at the naval vessels. These were the weapons of the mighty British Empire, the ships that could close down the American coast to foreign trade should London give the order. "We'll have to have our own navy if we ever expect to be a free people," John Turnbull called to them. "Now that it looks like Britain is driving the colonies to war, Americans will find out soon enough that the nation that controls the seas controls the commerce of the world. And any nation with a seacoast must have a navy if it hopes to remain free."

The British ships loomed larger and larger as the schooner swept toward them. Turnbull called the boys over, and Andrew and Nathan walked back across the steeply slanting deck to join him at the wheel. The powerfully-built master handed Andrew a long brass telescope. "Look at those warships, boys. I want you to be able to recognize them in the dark. Study their masts and rigging."

Andrew took the long instrument, opened it, spread his feet wide for balance, and steadied the lens. *That's the ship whose marines stole the gunpowder from the magazine* he thought to himself. This was the act that had set the whole Colony of Virginia in an uproar. Focusing first on the stern of the sleek and deadly vessel, he saw that an officer was looking directly at the *Morning Star* through his own telescope.

Andrew had a sinking sensation as he realized how helpless the *Morning Star* was in the presence of the fast, heavily armed warship. He turned the glass then on the *Magdelen's* masts, and began to study the shape of each in turn. Then he handed the telescope to Nathan.

"An officer is looking at us!" Nathan observed at once as he focused on the warship.

"I saw him," Andrew replied. "Hope he doesn't think we're suspicious."

"Don't worry," Turnbull said, "he's got no reason to bother us. But it's his job to study all the shipping in these waters, and that's what he's doing. Soon enough, I fear, he'll be ordered to stop any of our ships he can find. Especially the larger vessels."

Nathan continued to study the masts and rigging of the *Magdelen.* They looked at the hull. Finally he closed up the scope and handed it back to Turnbull, who took it in his free hand and set it in a rack beside the wheel.

"Would you recognize her again?" Turnbull asked.

"Yes, sir, I would," Nathan replied.

"So would I," Andrew said.

"Good. You never know when your lives may depend on it. And when it's dark, or when you're in a storm, you don't have much time to study such things. You've got to be able to recognize an enemy at once if you hope to escape."

Gradually, the two British warships fell behind the racing schooner. Both boys felt a sense of relief at this, and they began again to enjoy the fast pace of the *Morning Star* as it sliced through the water. Now the strong wind was driving the vessel past the port city of Yorktown, which lay to their right.

"There's Mr. Nelson's house," Andrew said, pointing to a fine brick home set on a rising hill close to the river. Both boys looked at the home of one of Virginia's most prominent men. Other homes lined the hill of the small town. Now the boys began to notice the rougher seas as they came into the broad waters of the Chesapeake Bay. In a short while the vessel swept by the town of Hampton and headed into the wide entrance that took them into the Atlantic Ocean.

Andrew and Nathan wandered forward and stood by the foremast. Thomas was at the bowsprit, splicing line. His bright teeth grinned in his dark face as the boys approached.

"Thomas!" Nathan exclaimed, "it's been weeks since we've been on this schooner!"

"Time you boys got back on board, then," Thomas said. "Before you forget all I've taught you about sailing this boat!"

"But it seems more dangerous, this time," Andrew replied thoughtfully. "Now that there's been fighting with the British. I sure hope Mr. Turnbull keeps an eye out for other British warships and turns toward shore if they start to come our way."

"I do too," Nathan replied. Nathan Edwards was almost fully grown, and already taller than most men. His thick brown hair was blowing in the wind. Like Andrew, he wore a long-sleeved canvass shirt and dark trousers. Each boy had his knife and tomahawk in his belt. The packs with the rest of their gear and extra clothes were in the small cabin below decks. They both loved making these voyages with John Turnbull, who made them work under Thomas as part of the crew.

Thomas was a good friend to the boys, and an excellent sailor, as well as a fine seafaring instructor. He'd worked for Turnbull for the past eight years, and his wife and five children lived in a house on Turnbull's property. An industrious Christian man, Thomas had worked and saved to purchase his own freedom, and then he'd purchased the freedom of his wife. Now he stepped forward with a coiled line in his hand, and began to secure two barrels in the bow of the ship.

Nathan glanced over at Andrew as the boys stood by the rail with their hands gripping the lines. "We'll have a lot to do in New York," he said thoughtfully.

"We sure will," Andrew agreed. "First, we help unload the ship and pack the cargo in Mr. Brown's wagons. Then we've got to talk with them about our fathers' letters, and learn all we can about their plans to trade by land if the British blockade the whole Atlantic coast."

"Don't forget," Nathan said, "we've also got to get their money for our cargo. Or rather, Mr. Turnbull has got to get it."

"He won't forget the money!" Thomas laughed. "And remember, we've got to load up with the stuff our Virginians have ordered from New York."

"It'll be mighty expensive trading by land," Nathan said thoughtfully, returning to that theme. "If the British navy blockades our coast, that'll send transportation prices sky high. Everything will cost more then." He watched a gull swoop close to the forward sail, then swerve away.

"It all depends on how many ships the British send, and when they send them, Father says," Andrew replied. "It'll take a while for England to gather their warships and bring them to our shores; their navy's already stretched all over the globe, even as far as India. They've got their warships in every seas where they've been fighting the French."

Twelve days later, however, in the busy harbor of New York, Andrew and Nathan learned that the British Navy was not so stretched that it had not been able to bring three of England's leading generals, and more soldiers, to the city of Boston. The two boys were closeted with the merchant, Horatio Brown, and his son Justin. The *Morning Star* had been unloaded, its cargo inventoried and paid for, and men were loading the boat now with cargo destined for Virginia. Turnbull and Thomas were at the dock supervising the loading, while Andrew and Nathan met with Horatio Brown and Justin in the large office in Brown's warehouse. Andrew and Nathan were listening with alarm to the news Mr. Brown was sharing with them.

"I guess you boys know that when the British raided Lexington and Concord, and fired on our militia, thousands of militia from other towns came from all over New England and bottled up the British army in Boston. But we've just learned that our militia units are almost out of gunpowder!" he said. "We've got to send them some, and right away. I've asked John Turnbull if you two can go with my son, Justin, to Cambridge, and take some gunpowder to our army."

Justin Brown was fifteen, the same height as Andrew, and had become a fast friend as he'd helped them with the unloading and reloading of the *Morning Star*. Like the two boys from Virginia, he too had been trained by his father to work in the shipping business. A steady, serious young man, he'd impressed Andrew and Nathan with his judgment and prudence. He sat beside his father as Horatio Brown put his suggestion to the two boys from Virginia.

Justin's father, Horatio Brown, was large, heavy-set, with just a fringe of gray hair above his ears. A genial man, he and Mrs. Brown had put up Andrew and Nathan and John Turnbull in their home for the past two days while Thomas had stayed with the schooner to guard it and its cargo. From Horatio Brown the Virginians had learned of the great gathering of American militia units from the New England colonies that had rushed to Boston after the Battle of Lexington.

"Then some of the other colonies sent militia to help Massachusetts?" Andrew asked, awed at this display of colonial unity in the face of British aggression.

"Yes, indeed! They came from all over, they did, from Rhode Island, from Connecticut, and from New Hampshire. To be honest, the minutemen of Massachusetts were probably the best trained. But those other colonies sent their men, ready to defend Massachusetts, and they're there now." He paused and lit his pipe. "The towns and villages just sent their men as soon as they'd learned of the British attack on Lexington and Concord. The militia regiments have all got Minute Men companies, and they can march in a hurry. But so too can the other companies, and there are hundreds of them. They're all around the city of Boston — Boston's an island connected to the mainland by a narrow neck of land — and they've got five thousand British soldiers bottled up in the city."

"What about the British ships?" Nathan had asked.

"They're in the bay all around the city, of course, with their guns trained on our towns. And that's how the British army is getting its food — by sea. Since the British blockaded Boston, our men have blockaded the British army in the town. They can't get any supplies from the countryside. They're existing on lousy rations from the fleet — dried beef, and moldy bread, from the barrels in their ships — and they're not happy at all. Serves 'em right!" he said.

But now, Brown told them, the colonial militia units were in bad shape too. "It's not food that they lack. They've got plenty of that. It's powder. And guns. They've got all kinds of weapons, whatever each family happened to own. But they're about out of gunpowder. Don't know how that happened — we've had several years to build up these militia units. I think they used it all up in practice firing, expecting to get more. And lots of 'em shot up almost all they had when they drove the Redcoats back from Lexington. But that's the problem now — they're out of powder."

"Then what would happen if the British would attack?" Andrew asked, alarmed.

"Our men would fire a few shots, then retreat, I guess," Brown said. "They sure can't fight without gunpowder. That's why we've got to send them some. Now, let me tell you what John Turnbull and I have decided to do."

He leaned over the table, and spread out a map drawn on heavy parchment. Andrew and Nathan and Justin leaned forward too. "Here's Boston," Brown pointed, thrusting his pencil at the map. "See how it's surrounded by water, except for this narrow neck of land?"

The boys nodded. Flies buzzed around them, and the boys brushed them away. New York was hot, they'd found, and the room, filled with its dusty ledgers and stacks of paper, was stifling.

"Here are our militia units," Brown continued, drawing his pencil around the circumference of land ringing the bay that surrounded Boston. "They're all around the city. But the bay and the rivers protect Boston from our militia — and protect our militia from those highly trained British soldiers, too!"

Brown leaned back and took a long drink of apple cider from the tankard beside him. The boys drank from their own mugs. They'd come to like this New York cider, which tasted different than what they'd been accustomed to in Virginia. Then Brown pointed at the map again.

"You can't sail near Boston, of course. The British ships would grab you. But you can sail to Newport, to the south of Boston, land the barrels of powder we've collected, and ride to Cambridge. Cambridge's just a few miles from the water that surrounds Boston. Our command and supply center is there. So is my business partner, Jeremiah Hanson. You boys can find him and give him the powder. He'll know how to distribute it to the army."

Brown glanced at Andrew and Nathan, and his eyes were troubled. Andrew realized suddenly that he wished he didn't have to ask them to go with the gunpowder. "Boys, I wouldn't ask you to do this, but it's an emergency. Don't go if you think you shouldn't. John Turnbull thinks that it's safe enough, and that your fathers would approve. But you two decide. Justin knows the way, and he can go by himself if he has to. But we'd sure like for you to go with him if you think it's right."

Andrew and Nathan looked at each other. Then Nathan replied. "If Mr. Turnbull says it's all right, then I think my father would want me to go."

"Mine would too, Mr. Brown," Andrew agreed. "As long as Mr. Turnbull approves." Andrew looked at Mr. Brown. "We're with Mr. Turnbull, sir, and our fathers would want us to trust his judgment. We'd be proud to help out the northern colonies if we could."

"Excellent!" Mr. Brown said, leaning back in his chair and beaming at the boys with great relief. "Here's what you'll do. We've got just a dozen barrels of powder right now. That's little enough — but our militia units around Boston need every barrel they can get! We've also got some barrels of flints, and shovels. And we've collected some muskets, and tents. John Turnbull's loading all this on the *Morning Star*. You boys will go with him, and Justin will join you. The boat will set sail for Newport in the morning, and unload the barrels there."

He took another deep drink from the cool cider, then wiped his sweating face with his sleeve. "Man, it's hot in here!"

He leaned forward again and continued his instructions. "In Newport, Justin will take you to meet our agent, Mr. Jones, and get a wagon. Maybe two, if Jones has supplies to send. You boys will ride with Justin, ahead of the wagons, and get to Cambridge as fast as you can. There you'll look up my partner Jeremiah Hanson, and lead him back to meet the wagons. He'll see that they're unloaded. Then you three can ride back to Newport — don't wait for the wagons — meet the *Morning Star*, and sail back here. Then you two will go back to Virginia on the schooner."

Brown looked at the map again. "Our militia regiments have got the British troops bottled up. But our men have **got** to have powder. If they don't get it, they'll have to retreat. And the British can attack any town in Massachusetts they want to!"

He looked at the Virginians again. "I sure appreciate your willingness to help! If you boys go along, the drivers can stay with the wagons and guard the powder while you two and Justin search for Mr. Hanson. I'm grateful."

☆ **CHAPTER FOUR** ☆

"WE'VE GOT TO FORTIFY BUNKER HILL!"

Several days later Andrew, Nathan, and Justin rode into Cambridge, Massachusetts. They'd left the two wagons with their drivers some miles behind, and hurried ahead to find Brown's partner, Jeremiah Hanson. "There'll be many soldiers and merchants there," Brown had told them. "Go to the army headquarters and ask for Jeremiah Hanson. Don't let anyone else know what your wagons are bringing — some eager quartermasters might steal the powder and supplies for their own militia units! Just search for Hanson 'till you find him."

The winds had been against them for part of the voyage, and the *Morning Star* had taken longer to reach Newport, Rhode Island, then they had expected. Mr. Jones and the wagons were waiting for them when they arrived, however, and a gang of men made short work of transferring the cargo from the schooner. Jones was a tall, thin man with a perpetual frown, and he was most efficient. While the workers unloaded the schooner, he gave the boys the latest information about the situation in Cambridge.

"Just find the army headquarters and ask for Jeremiah Hanson," Mr. Jones had told them. "Cambridge isn't a large town. You'll track him down. But be sure you get him before you bring the wagons into town. We don't want the wrong units getting this shipment!"

Now the three boys rode into Cambridge, dodging scores of armed men in the streets, riding around supply wagons and marching militia units. Noncoms were shouting orders to the various militia companies, dogs were barking, drums were beating, and the boys' hearts pounded with excitement as they held their nervous horses to a walk through this frenzied activity. At a cross street, Justin spotted a sergeant who was directing the incoming militia companies. Riding over to the sergeant, Justin asked for directions to the army headquarters.

"Down that street," the sergeant pointed. "You'll see guards outside the building they're using — it's on the right." Justin thanked him and the three boys turned their horses in the direction he'd indicated. In a few minutes they'd found the house they were looking for.

"This is it!" Justin said. Stepping from the saddle he handed the reins to Nathan. "I'll go inside and find Mr. Hanson."

Justin walked quickly through the door, but was stopped at once by a sergeant seated at a desk. The man's hands were filled with papers. Quickly Justin told him his errand. The sergeant turned his head and called through an open door. "Private, direct this boy to Mr. Hanson."

A lean man in butternut trousers and shirt walked over and led Justin into a side room. Here, a powerfully built man in dark coat and trousers was seated at a desk by the window, pen in hand, poring over the papers before him. Justin wondered to himself if armies had to have as many men with pens as with guns! Everyone he'd seen in this headquarters so far held only pens — no weapons at all!

"Justin Brown!" Hanson called out as he spotted the boy. "What are you doing here? Doesn't your father know that we're about to have a war?" But his question was softened by the kind smile that wreathed his wide tanned face as he rose from his desk and clasped Justin's hand in his strong grip.

"Yes, sir, he does, Mr. Hanson," Justin replied. "And that's why he sent me. But can I talk to you outside?"

"Certainly," Hanson replied, "lead the way, Justin." Justin led the merchant outside, and introduced him to Andrew and Nathan who had dismounted and were standing holding the reins of the three horses. Justin told Mr. Hanson of the two wagons with their supplies for the army.

"Gunpowder! And flints!" Hanson exclaimed. Then he looked around quickly. Lowering his voice, he asked, "Where is it? We're desperately short of powder, Justin. We've got almost ten thousand militiamen surrounding Boston, and most of them are just about out of powder."

"Yes, sir," Justin answered, "that's what father said. The wagons are just a few miles out of town, heading this way. But the drivers won't come in town 'till we tell them to. Father said to wait until you came and led us to the right units."

"Good for him!" Hanson said. He stood a moment in thought, and the three boys regarded him with interest. Dressed in dark trousers, with a long dark coat, and a white shirt, he looked almost elegant compared to many of the casually dressed militiamen thronging the small town.

"We've just had a stormy meeting," Hanson said finally. Glancing around to see that no one was within hearing, he continued.

"We've learned that the English General Howe plans to attack our command center here in Cambridge. To do that, he's leading an amphibious attack from Boston across the water to Dorchester. Then he'll swing around to the north, rolling up our right flank and striking at our center, here in this town. We've got fifteen regiments of militia here protecting Cambridge, with General Artemas Ward in command, but we're facing a major crisis."

A group of militiamen rushed into the house then, and Hanson paused. Two messengers ran shouting out the door, calling for troops to muster. Hanson's face grew solemn. "While General Howe strikes our army's right flank at Dorchester Point, General Clinton will lead another amphibious attack on Charleston, just across the water opposite Boston. That's on our left flank. Then the two British columns will attack Cambridge from both directions at once. We're in the middle right here, and if the British regulars attack our militia units from both flanks at the same time we'll be in a heap of trouble."

A passing militiaman fired his musket, apparently by accident, but the sudden shot spooked the horses the boys held. Only by the greatest exertions were they able to hold the frightened animals, and bring them under control. While the other militiamen laughed, a corporal yelled blistering comments at the hapless man.

Hanson grinned at the incident. Then his face became serious again, and he continued his explanation to the three boys. "So our leaders have planned to surprise the British by fortifying the high ground that overlooks Boston, before the redcoats themselves attack us! But I don't know if our plan is a good one. Like I said, our army is almost out of powder. That's a terrible situation for an army to find itself in. But General Israel Putnam has just persuaded our other militia leaders that fortifying Bunker Hill will spoil the British plans, and halt their attack. Bunker Hill's a hill above Charleston. That way, our artillery can command Boston itself, and shell any landing the British attempt."

"Yes, sir," Justin replied, puzzled at the merchant's concern. "That'll stop that attack from the left, I guess?"

"General Putnam thinks so," Hanson said. "But the trouble is, as Dr. Warren and General Ward argued, to fortify Bunker Hill our men have got to march across a narrow neck of land between two rivers, the Mystic and the Charles. The British have got warships in those rivers. Those ships could fire at our men as they crossed, or land troops behind them and bottle them up on that peninsula. They'd be trapped. Dr. Warren and General Ward argued and argued, but old Israel Putnam finally beat them down."

Hanson stood quietly for a moment, deep in thought. Drums suddenly began beating, and more men were shouting in the streets. The boys looked up and saw a large unit of militia marching toward them, raising a cloud of dust. Their horses began again to fidget nervously at the sound of the drums, and the boys gripped the reins to keep them from bolting.

"Well, what's decided is decided!" Jeremiah Hanson said finally, his kindly face grim at the dangers that faced them. "It's not my decision. What I've got to do is get this powder to the right men, and I think General Putnam's the man to ask. Wait here — I'll go in and tell him what you've brought, then I'll ride with you to the wagons and lead them in." He walked rapidly into the house.

A group of militiamen came marching by, behind three drummers. The boys' horses snorted, and jerked back their heads at the noise of the drums, so that the boys had all they could do to hold them.

"We've got to get these horses out of town!" Andrew said. "This noise is driving them wild!" All three mounted now, the better to control the nervous animals.

Just as the militia unit passed, Mr. Hanson hurried out the door and walked over to the hitch rail in front of the house where several horses were tethered. He untied, then mounted a large black gelding, and wheeled the eager animal into the dusty road. "Lead me to the wagons!" he called.

The three boys whirled their mounts and led Hanson at a gallop out of the town.

Several hours later, after dark had fallen, the four tired riders rode their mounts back to the army headquarters. The building was ablaze with lanterns, and men were constantly rushing in and out the front door. Dismounting, they tethered their horses to the rail in front of the house. Andrew, Nathan, and Justin hurried after Mr. Hanson as he strode into the front door.

Hanson let the boys through the entrance hall, to a large room illumined with a dozen tall candles. Entering, the boys saw a large uniformed soldier standing at the window, looking out. The man turned at their entrance, and Hanson introduced them to the famous General Putnam. "These are the boys who brought us the gunpowder, General," he said, naming each in turn.

The General was ecstatic at the supply of powder, small as it was, and thanked the boys profusely.

"It's precious little powder, I'm afraid, General," Hanson said, "but it's all that we could gather on such short notice."

"That's true," General Putnam said, "but it's more than we had before these boys arrived! We thank you."

General Putnam was a big man, powerfully muscled, with a voice to match the size of his muscles. "He's magnificently mounted," Hanson had told the boys earlier, "and he's got in his saddle holsters a fine pair of pistols taken from the English Major John Pitcairn at the battle of Lexington. Pitcairn's horse ran off into American militia units," Hanson had said with a smile, "and old Israel Putnam got the pistols!"

Now, the boys looked in awe at the Colonial leader standing before them. He seemed lost in thought for a moment.

"Hanson," the General said suddenly. "I can use these young men as messengers. Will you lend them to me for the next few hours?"

"As long as you keep them away from the fighting, General," Hanson replied cautiously. "They're in my care, and I can't endanger them."

"I'll keep them out of the fighting," Putnam said, "we've got enough men for that. But I do need messengers to alert our militia units, as well as to keep me informed of what's happening. We've moving out tonight, to build fortifications overlooking Boston — before the British wake up tomorrow morning. I want to send these boys with the advance units, so they can bring back messages from their commanders. We've got to know how our fortifying work proceeds. If the British discover us before the work is completed, there's no telling what they might do. They could attack in a hurry, before we're ready. I've got to have mounted messengers with those units who can be spared to get information back to me at once."

General Putnam looked keenly at the three boys standing before him. "We're going to fortify Bunker Hill, as I said," he told them. "The British think they're going to surprise us by landing at Charleston. But they're the ones who are in for a surprise! When they see our fortifications and guns, they'll know they have to change their plans!"

"Let's go outside," he said crisply. Without waiting for a reply, he strode past them out of the room, down the hall, through the door and into the darkness of the yard. Hanson and the three boys hurried after him and joined him beside a bonfire.

Wagons were all around them, wagons filled with tools for fortifying Bunker Hill. These included shovels, bundles of sticks to use as shields from musket balls, and empty barrels ready to be filled with dirt to absorb British bullets.

"We're waiting for Colonel Prescott," General Putnam explained to Hanson and the boys. "Technically, as General, I outrank him. But I'm in command of Connecticut militia, and Prescott's got Massachusetts men — and we're in Massachusetts! So he's the logical man to command this operation. Besides, he's a splendid soldier and leader. In fact, he's such an outstanding soldier that the British offered him a permanent commission in their army after we beat the French at Louis-bourg. He refused it, thank the Lord! He's the right man for us now."

Suddenly a rider galloped through the yard, scattering a group of militiamen.

"Keep your horse in the street!" the General yelled angrily in his powerful voice. Then he turned to the three boys. "You men had better get on your horses before one of these reckless fools scatters them for you!"

The boys mounted at once. Hanson and General Putnam stood before them. Andrew and Nathan held their rifles, resting these across their saddles. Over their shoulders they'd slung their powder horns and bullet pouches. Justin had brought his father's carbine, a short-barreled rifle, and he too had powder horn and bullet pouch slung over his shoulder. And, like the Virginians, he was skilled with the rifled gun.

"Take your weapons with you, boys," Hanson had told them when they'd led him to the wagons. "I don't want you to be riding around unarmed. Not tonight. Not so close to the British army."

Suddenly there was the sound of another galloping horse. A rider hauled his mount to a hurried stop just before Putnam. "Colonel Prescott's coming, General," he said crisply.

"How many men has he got?" Putnam asked at once.

"About twelve hundred. They're minutemen mostly, I think."

"Splendid," Putnam replied. He turned to Hanson and the boys. "Massachusetts has got thousands of men in companies that train regularly, and are ready to march at a moment's notice. And each company's got a special unit that can mobilize even quicker. That's why they're called 'Minutemen'. They're as well trained as any of the British regiments in Boston. And they're better shots. Especially the rifle men!" He spoke again to the messenger. "Tell the men at the wagons to get ready to move."

Then they heard the tramp of Prescott's marching men. Soon the long column wound into the town and came to a halt. Now everything seemed to happen at once! Colonel Prescott and another officer came up to General Putnam as the wagons began to pull into columns.

The darkness of the night was relieved only by bonfires and torches, but these threw light over the group of officers. Jeremiah Hanson spoke quietly to the three boys. "See that man with Colonel Prescott? That's Colonel Richard Gridley. He's as fine an engineering officer as the colonies have! In fact, he so distinguished himself against the French that the British Government made him a colonel with a pension and gave him three thousand acres of land in New Hampshire."

"What did he do?" Andrew asked.

"We were fighting the French on the Plains of Abraham, in Canada. It began to look like we'd have to retreat. Colonel Gridley got some men to haul a couple of cannons up a hill overlooking the fighting, a hill that the French thought couldn't be climbed. Those guns opened fire, and their shooting was so deadly that the French lines fell back, and our forces drove them from the field. Gridley's a great officer! In fact, there aren't two finer officers on this continent than Prescott and Gridley! I must say, boys, this encourages me vastly!"

Then the conference ended. Prescott called to his officers, gave his commands, and the long column began to move. But General Putnam, flanked now by Colonel Prescott and Colonel Gridley, turned to Hanson and the boys and waved them over. The General introduced the two officers to Hanson, then said, "Colonel Prescott needs messengers to go with him, Hanson. He'd like to borrow these three young men for a few hours."

General Putnam introduced the three boys to Colonel Prescott. "I sure could use you men," the lean officer said. "We've got to let the General here know just when we've got our fortifications ready. And, if anything goes wrong, and the British make moves before our army's ready, we've got to tell him right away."

The boys looked eagerly at Mr. Hanson. He paused a moment, then asked them. "How about it, boys? You don't have to do this, you know."

"We'd be glad to help, sir," Justin said. Nathan and Andrew nodded their heads in agreement.

Hanson stood in thought. Then he replied. "Well, Colonel, they're eager to go with you. I'm responsible for them. Just see that they stay away from any fighting."

"I'll certainly do that," Prescott said with a smile. "I'll have them all back here by noon."

Jeremiah Hanson turned to the three excited boys. "Take care, now. Meet me here when you return."

"Yes, sir!" they replied.

"I'll see that those supplies reach your units, General," Hanson said to Putnam. Waving to the boys, he rode off.

"Follow us, boys," Prescott said. "We've got to fortify Bunker Hill before sunup." He and the General and Colonel Gridley put their horses into a trot. The boys did the same, and the six horsemen quickly passed the marching men and rode ahead of them toward Bunker Hill.

It was the sixteenth day of June, in the Year of Our Lord, 1775.

CHAPTER FIVE

"WE'LL FORTIFY BREED'S HILL INSTEAD!"

The horsemen rode across Charleston Neck, the narrow spit of land between the Charles and Mystic Rivers. Lights from houses across the way, and lights from the British warships, flickered on the water. Once across the narrow neck of land, the riders slowed their horses, and turned off the road, walking their mounts carefully in the darkness. The officers began to study the terrain. They rode between the mainland and the town of Charleston ahead of them, and it soon became apparent to the three boys that the officers were puzzled.

"They didn't tell me there were three hills here," the General said. "Which one's Bunker Hill?"

"I don't know, General," Colonel Gridley replied, "but I do know that we'd better fortify the one closest to Boston so our cannons will reach their ships and batteries."

They struck a light and studied the map Colonel Gridley held in his hands. "That one you're talking about is Breed's Hill, Gridley. Bunker Hill's over there," the General said.

"My orders are to fortify Bunker Hill, General," Prescott said quietly. "I wasn't told to fortify Breed's Hill."

"But it's the key to the whole position," Gridley replied. "It's closer to the river — and to Boston. Our guns on that hill could endanger not only the British fortifications in Boston but also any British ships in the waters between. Shot fired from this height would go right into their decks and hulls."

And now the three boys were treated to a remarkable experience as the officers argued over the tactical situation. For the conditions had changed. Originally, the men had been ordered to fortify Bunker Hill so as to threaten the British in Boston and render their position untenable. Arrived at the scene, however, they'd found another hill that seemed more suitable to the intent of their instructions. The question that faced them was this: should they carry out the letter of their orders, and fortify Bunker Hill, or should they — as Colonel Gridley argued — fortify the hill nearest Boston and the river, which was Breed's Hill. This hill was closer to Boston, and thus, Colonel Gridley argued, more suitable for the accomplishment of their mission. From this hill, the American guns could reach more British targets than they could from Bunker Hill.

Gridley finally won the day. The other agreed to fortify Breed's Hill, closer to Boston. "All right," Prescott agreed. "I'll do it, Gridley. Breed's Hill it is. I'll take the responsibility, too. But I'll also have some men begin fortifying Bunker Hill as well. Andrew, ride back and tell the leading units what we're doing. Then lead them here."

"Yes, sir," Andrew said, wheeling his horse. But General Putnam spoke before he rode off. "Wait, Andrew, I'll go with you." He said to Colonel Prescott. "I'm going back to headquarters. We've still got to be ready to fight the other British column on our right if they land from the ships and march on

Cambridge." He turned his horse and put the big steed into a run, with Andrew running his mount beside him.

Colonel Gridley turned to Nathan and Justin. "Come with me, boys," he said. "I want to study where the trenches will be built, and I want you to see what I'm doing so you can answer my mens' questions if I'm on another part of the field."

For the next hour the boys accompanied the officer as he pointed out his plan for the fort. "We're building a redoubt, boys," he told them. "It's going to be 160 yards long — forty yards to each side. It'll cover our men if the British attack, because we'll make the walls six feet high. That six feet of dirt will soak up any musket balls the British fire at us. We'll also have barrels of dirt to stop their cannonballs should the British fire their cannons. Our men will be covered as they fire at any attacking Redcoats. And we'll have our own cannons to dominate the British positions in Boston — if they get here in time, that is."

"Can our soldiers build a fort before sunup?" Andrew asked incredulously.

"These aren't really soldiers, Andrew," Gridley said with a smile the boy couldn't see in the darkness. "They're farmers, mostly. They could build *anything* before sunup! Work in the fields is what they do all day long. They can build anything, anywhere! You just watch!"

And build they did. Arriving at the spot, the men stacked their muskets in the darkness, took the shovels that had been brought for them, and fell to with a will, digging along the lines Gridley had marked. They worked steadily through the early hours of the morning. Once Prescott sent Justin and Nathan back to General Putnam, asking for more gunpowder. But they had to return with the news that none was yet available.

Prescott received this information without a word. "Go get a couple of hours sleep, boys," he said. "I want you rested when the sun comes up."

Just then, Andrew rode up. He'd been detached by General Putnam to lead another column of militiamen across the Neck to Breed's Hill. He dismounted stiffly, and joined Nathan and Justin as they led their horses over to a group of wagons and tethered them. Then the three tired boys curled up in one of the supply wagons that had brought a load of shovels to the soldiers, and were soon fast asleep.

But it seemed as if they'd only closed their eyes when the sound of cannons firing brought them quickly awake.

"What's that?" Andrew asked, leaping to his feet and reaching for his rifle. He was surprised to see the faint light of very early morning.

"The British have seen us!" a nearby militiaman replied. "They're firing their ships' guns!"

Below the hill, on the British ship *Lively,* a startled British marine had peered through the early morning mist to see the American fortifications on the hill above the river. Shocked — those fortifications had not been there the night before! — he'd called for the officer of the watch. This man peered in astonishment at the fortifications, and yelled at once for the *Lively's* captain.

Captain Thomas Bishop leaped from his hammock in the small cabin at the stern of the ship, threw on his clothes, rushed out on deck, and raced up the steps to the quarter-deck. There he found the excited Marine sentry, who pointed out to the captain the American earthworks on the hill above them. Utterly astounded to see such a professional fortification thrown up overnight, Captain Bishop studied the redoubt through his telescope. Then he called for the drummer to beat the crew to battle stations.

The drums shattered the still air with their stirring staccato command, and the suddenly roused crew tumbled from their hammocks. Sleepy sailors rushed out on deck, and the gunners ran to the cannons on the starboard side of the ship. Men dashed up with barrels of powder, cannon balls were brought from the magazines, the long matches were lit, and at the captain's orders the ten cannon on that side of the ship blasted in unison.

The thunderous sound of the guns shocked everyone — the people in Boston, the crews of the British ships, and the American militiamen digging feverishly on the hill across from Boston. Here, a militiaman yelled in fright, "A British ship's firing at us!"

Andrew, Nathan, and Justin grabbed their rifles and ran toward the crowds of militiamen who'd thrown themselves to the ground when the British cannon had begun firing at the dirt walls of their redoubt. As the militiamen saw the red balls from the ship fall short of their position, however, they rose to their feet and watched the warship.

The boys rushed up and stood amid the militia. They saw far below them on the water the warship firing furiously. Puffs of white smoke billowed from it's side, followed by the high curving flight of the cannon balls heading for the American positions.

"That little ship won't hurt this fort!" one of the men called out derisively.

"Not unless they raise their aim," Colonel Prescott said soberly.

On His Majesty's ship *Somerset,* a huge ship-of-the-line carrying 64 cannon, Admiral Samuel Graves was shocked from slumber by the explosion of the *Lively's* guns. Tumbling from his cot he staggered to the cabin door and bellowed for the sentry.

"Who's firing those guns?" he raged.

In a moment the sentry had the answer. "The *Lively,* sir. They're firing broadsides."

"I didn't order them to fire!" the Admiral shouted. "Signal their Captain to cease at once!"

"Yes, sir," the sentry replied. He ran to the quarter-deck and passed the message to the ship's captain. At once the captain commanded the signal men to order the *Lively* to cease firing.

But it took several minutes for the signal men to get their flags ready. In the meantime, the broadsides from the *Lively* continued to shatter the morning air. Finally, the men on the Admiral's flagship had the signals ready. These were hoisted up the tall mast.

On board the *Lively,* a midshipman perched high in the rigging of the ship peered through his telescope and took in the signal from the Admiral's flagship. Snapping shut the brass instrument, he slung this by its cord over his shoulder, then nimbly threw himself over the crosstree and slid down the rope rigging to the deck so many feet below. Leaping the final steps, he landed on deck and ran back to Captain Bishop who stood on the quarter-deck with his telescope trained on the American fortifications.

"The flagship orders 'Cease firing', Captain."

"What?" Captain Bishop replied, lowering the telescope through which he'd been observing the fall of the cannonballs. He swore in disgust, then turned to the lieutenant standing by the ladder to the main deck and called, "Lieutenant, order the guns to cease firing."

The deck shook with the violence of another volley from the ship's cannons. Clouds of smoke pierced with flame shot from the side of the vessel as the thunder of the guns deafened the men on deck. Sailors then ran the guns back from the portholes through which they'd fired, thrust long poles with wet cloth on the ends down the gun barrels to extinguish any remaining sparks, then rammed in canvass bags of gunpowder. After this, a cannon ball was shoved into each gun and packed tight against the powder. Even as the Lieutenant yelled for the firing to cease, the guns were run out again so that the barrels protruded through the square holes in the ship's sides, ready for another volley.

But the command to cease halted the process. The gunners drew back with their lighted fuses and waited for further orders. They wiped the sweat from their red faces, thankful for the respite from the frantic loading, running out the guns through the firing ports, firing, hauling the heavy guns back in, and re-loading.

Back on the *Somerset*, Admiral Graves had finally reached the quarter-deck. "What made that madman fire his guns like that?" he yelled angrily at the ship's captain.

The captain handed the admiral his telescope. "The Americans have fortified the hills above us, Admiral. They've built a redoubt during the night. Guns from that redoubt can destroy our ships with plunging fire — if we don't knock out their guns first."

"A redoubt? They've built a redoubt in one night? Impossible!" the admiral exclaimed, taking the telescope and peering through it at the American positions. For a long moment he stared at the fortification on the hill. Then he swore, snapped the telescope shut, and turned to the ship's captain with a hard glare.

"No troops in the world could do that in one night! How long has that fort been there? Why didn't your lookouts report this before?"

"It wasn't there before, Admiral," the captain assured him. "The Americans built that last night."

The Admiral's jaw fell slack with shock. The naval officers knew at once that if the Colonials were to place heavy cannons on that hill, every British ship in the harbor would be in mortal danger from the plunging fire that could pierce the decks and go through the vessel's wooden hulls, opening their bottoms to the deadly seas. Again Admiral Graves raised the telescope to his eyes, and focused on Breed's Hill. "Order the fleet to commence firing on the American fortifications!" he bellowed. "Blow that rebel fort to pieces!"

The naval officers knew full well that with guns on the hill above the bay and the city, the Americans could shell not only the ships in the harbor but also the army fortifications in Boston. And they could severely damage and maybe frustrate the British plan to land troops on shore and march to attack the American forces defending Cambridge. Now the officers grinned with satisfaction that the admiral had ordered the fleet to destroy the American fort.

The captain yelled the admiral's order to his lieutenant. The lieutenant yelled to the signal man. Soon, sailors were hauling signal flags up the lines to the top of the mast. Signalmen and midshipmen on the other ships whose duty it was to watch the Admiral's signals read the flags and called down to the officers on the decks below them. Meanwhile, the captain of the *Somerset* turned to his first lieutenant and ordered him to bring the ship to action.

Shouted commands burst upon the morning air, the drums began their stirring beat, and three hundred men poured onto the deck of the *Somerset*, racing to their battle stations. The big guns were run out, powder and cannon balls were rushed to the guns, fires for the guns' fuses were lit, and soon the ship shook with the mighty thunder of the first broadside. Smoke pierced with flame burst from the ship's side.

In a few minutes the entire fleet was firing furiously at the fort on the high hill in an awe-inspiring spectacle of raw naval power. Rolling clouds of smoke flew from the sides of the warships, red hot cannonballs climbed high into the air, then fell in their graceful curving descent to the ground below. Up on the hill, the Americans fell to the ground once again as the ships in the harbor, as well as those in the Charles and Mystic Rivers, fired their broadsides in furious bombardment.

In the city of Boston, and in the village of Charleston just below the American redoubt, citizens poured out of their houses to watch the astounding spectacle of the mighty naval cannonade. They saw the clouds of white smoke shoot from the ships' guns and float across the harbor. They heard the cries of the frantic hundreds of screaming sea-birds who now circled madly in the sky above the bay. And on shore, British army units were roused and called to form ranks. Dogs howled furiously as the sound of over a hundred cannons pounded their ears. Horses neighed wildly in the city and bucked desperately at the thunder of the big guns. Several panicked mounts broke free at the dreadful noise and galloped frantically through the streets, pursued by packs of madly barking dogs.

But to the American militiamen on Breed's Hill, it became apparent once again that the British shot was not reaching the fort itself. The hill was too high above the water, and the cannonballs were falling to the sloping ground short of the American position. Unwisely, some of the Americans decided that these cannonballs posed no danger, and ran out among them. But the red-hot balls had terrible momentum when they struck the ground, and some came bounding upward toward the militiamen gathered on the hill. Suddenly, several men were wounded, and several more were killed when these balls careened into them. The militiamen fell back, and stopped their digging.

Then a cannon ball hit one of the militiamen just in front of the redoubt, killing him instantly. The victim's blood splattered Colonel Prescott who was standing beside him. Shocked at the violent death of their comrade, a group of militia turned to flee.

But at these first signs of panic among his men, Colonel Prescott jumped up on the parapet and waved his sword. "See how close they come to hitting me!" he shouted, as he walked back and forth on the top of the fortification, in plain sight of the furiously firing British guns.

Other officers leaped up on the parapet to join the gallant Colonel, encouraging the men. This broke the spell of fear that had fallen on the militiamen. Cheering their officers, they came out from behind the dirt wall and continued building the fortifications. Wielding their shovels with vigor, joking among themselves, they made the earth fly. Soon another wall of packed dirt came into being, stretching from the back of the fort, down toward the river away from Boston, thus covering the left flank of the American position.

"Nathan!" Colonel Prescott called, jumping down from the parapet now that his men were back at work.

"Yes, sir," the boy replied, rushing to the colonel's side.

"Ride to General Ward. Give him this note. Tell him we've got to have more powder! Some of my men only have enough for a dozen shots!"

"Yes, sir," Nathan replied. He ran to his horse, threw on the saddle, and rode back toward the peninsula that connected Charleston to the mainland. As he rode across the narrow causeway he saw with alarm that British ships in the river to his right, and in the harbor to his left, could devastate any American reinforcements if they chose to. Their cannons could reach the low ground with ease. And this causeway was the only way the Americans could approach, or retreat from Charleston! Now he understood why some of the American officers had protested marching their men out to fortify Bunker Hill; for if the British acted with tactical wisdom, and landed on the causeway behind the Americans instead of making a frontal attack on the fort, the militiamen would be cut off!

Nathan put his horse into a gallop as he reached the mainland, passing a troop of militia marching in loose formation toward Bunker Hill. Glancing behind him, he saw that Bunker Hill, too, was being fortified to resist British attack. The cannonading from the warships and floating batteries still pounded his ears as he galloped toward Cambridge.

Would battle break out before he could return to Breed's Hill?

If it did, how would Andrew and Justin escape the fighting?

☆ **CHAPTER SIX** ☆

THE BRITISH GENERALS

Major General Thomas Gage was in charge of the British forces in North America. Gage was a large man, who had spent years in the American Colonies. He had led the British advance forces under General Braddock when that army had been almost annihilated by an ambush of French and Indians in the forest. Rising in rank nevertheless, Gage had presented a friendly attitude to the Americans, and many trusted him. They did not know that in his letters to his superiors in London he had urged the sternest measures, pressing them to put down the beginnings of American efforts at independence before the colonists could arm for war.

As Commander of the British forces in Massachusetts, Gage ruled over the captive port of Boston. He had just presided over the council of war in which his generals had decided to attack the American forces surrounding Boston from each flank, drive them backward, and crush them at their headquarters in Cambridge.

Now, shocked awake by the firing of the British ships' guns, General Gage dressed hastily and called for his chief officers to assemble. As the generals gathered, an aide rushed in to tell Gage that the Americans had fortified the hills above Charleston, and that cannons from those hills could threaten not only

Boston but the British ships in the harbor as well. The General was shocked by this news.

Major General Henry Clinton arrived first. Clinton's father had been a British admiral, later Governor of New York, and General Clinton had been raised in that city. He'd entered the army by buying an officer's commission at the age of thirteen. After an undistinguished career, he'd nevertheless earned a reputation as a planner, and had been sent by King George to North America to assist in putting down the budding movement toward independence. He came quickly into the room, and General Gage waved him to a chair.

Then General John Burgoyne rushed in. Burgoyne was an interesting man, a genuine soldier as well as a writer of plays and a member of Parliament. He was most unusual for the British Army of that age in that he demanded that his officers and noncoms treat the soldiers under their command with genuine consideration, as human beings. The troops loved him.

General William Howe was the last to arrive. Tall, well-built, with dark complexion and brooding black eyes, Howe was the most famous soldier in the room. He'd earned a reputation for courage and brilliant tactical skill in England's wars against the French. Yet he was a firm supporter of the Americans, and had earned their love and respect. He'd also stated that the colonial cause was just, and that he would not accept a position in the army sent to subdue them.

However, when the King had offered Howe a position in the army sent to do just that, Howe had reversed himself. He'd arrived in Boston and promptly devised a plan for the quick destruction of the American army. "Defeat their military forces quickly," he'd urged, "then offer them generous terms of peace. Most of the colonists are loyal subjects of our King. Dispose of their ring-leaders, and the populace will once again be peaceful subjects."

Two more men entered the room. Brigadier, the Earl of Percy was a slender man, a very brave and competent soldier. It was he who had so skillfully led the relief expedition which had rescued the retreating British soldiers from the American militia at Lexington and Concord just two months before. With him came Brigadier Robert Pigot, another renowned fighting man.

General Gage began the meeting by sketching out the situation to the assembled officers. "We've got to take that redoubt before its guns can damage our ships!" he concluded decisively.

General Clinton suggested at once that he take 500 men by small boats and land them in the town of Charleston. "Then, I'll march them in front of the American positions on the top of Breed's and Bunker Hill, to the narrow piece of land that connects the isthmus with the mainland — what they call the 'Neck.' I'll cut off the Americans in their fortifications from retreating, and block any efforts to reinforce 'em from the mainland. We'll just starve them into surrendering!" he said quietly. "That causeway is their only way of retreat to the mainland. Block that, and we'll have them trapped."

This, of course, is the very thing Colonels Gridley and Prescott had feared, and had argued with General Putnam about. But they had been over-ruled: Putnam was determined to fortify the hills and threaten the British fleet and their forts in Boston.

General Gage shook his head. "Gentlemen, will we land men only to put them between enemy forces on two sides? They could be attacked simultaneously by more colonials from the mainland and from those at Bunker Hill and Breed's Hill as well. They'd be overwhelmed by a double-sided assault."

General Howe spoke then, with an air of calm certainty. "We don't have the proper boats for a quick amphibious landing, General." Howe was experienced in amphibious landings, as the other generals present were not, and his argument gave General Clinton pause.

General Howe and General Gage then began to discuss a frontal attack on the American fortifications.

General Clinton was appalled. "But there's no need for us to send our soldiers against those entrenchments!" he insisted. "We don't have enough troops in Boston to waste on such tactics. By landing on the neck of the peninsula, we'll have them trapped. Our ships close to shore will wipe out any attack they make on the soldiers we land. The Americans will try to break out, or try to attack from the mainland with other troops. When they see how many men they lose to our ships guns, they'll have to surrender! Our army is too small for us to waste men unnecessarily by making a frontal attack on fortified positions!"

"I agree, General," Gage replied ponderously, "that we don't want to take unnecessary casualties. But there's another point we've got to consider. Those colonists are in rebellion. Rebellion against our King. They've got to be taught a lesson. A severe lesson. A lesson that the whole Empire will understand. We've **got** to prove to them that it's hopeless for our colonies to rebel; that they'll suffer disaster if they try; and that our forces can and will destroy them if they are so foolish to attempt it."

He pointed to the map on the table. "Look at the American position. It's high on those two hills, above that little village of Charleston. Both hills are in sight of the city of Boston. The whole population of Boston will see what happens to those American units that have dared to threaten the British army. The whole city will see the dreadful whipping those rebel militia will receive from the bayonets of British Regulars. Their newspapers will spread the news throughout the American Colonies — and throughout the British Empire. *That*'s why we've got to attack those rebels in plain sight of the city. To teach them a lesson! To prove that rebellion against the King is futile! And costly! He pounded the table with his fist and glared around the room.

General Howe agreed. "General Gage is right, Gentlemen," he said quietly, dark eyes gleaming in his handsome face. Tall, powerfully built, his presence exuded power — and confidence. "Here's how we can do it," Howe said, scraping his chair closer to the table and pointing to the map. "We'll land at Morton's Point, on the tip of the peninsula. If the rebels attack us while we're landing our troops, the ships' guns will fire grapeshot at them and wipe them out before they can reach our men on the beach."

The other scarlet-coated leaders nodded agreement. Grape shot — scores of musket balls packed into cannons, in place of the single heavy cannon ball — were devastating against soldiers in the field. When fired with a full charge of powder, the musket balls spread out as they left the cannons and swept like deadly horizontal hail against soldiers in the open. No troops could stand against massed cannons firing grapeshot.

"I repeat," Howe said, "we can land our forces at Morton's Point, at the tip of the peninsula, just across from our docks in Boston. Morton's Point is only half a mile from the hills the Americans have fortified, so there's no danger of our men being ambushed when we land. We'll deploy on the shore, and send a column of light infantry to our right along the Mystic River. That's to the north of the American position, and on their left flank as they face our landing. That column will get into the rear of the American forces. Raw troops panic when they're threatened from the rear. Then our troops in front of their redoubt will simply attack when the rebels flee, and we'll catch them between two fires. We'll rout them. Then we'll continue with our plan to march on Cambridge from both sides and destroy the American army. This rebellion will be over in a day." He sat back and waited for the other men to respond.

"General," Clinton asked, still opposed to the idea of a frontal attack on the entrenched rebel militia, "what if the Americans inside that redoubt don't panic and run when they're outflanked? What if they remain, and fight from behind their fort? Our soldiers will have to attack them from the open fields."

"I see no problem, General," Howe replied with a smile. "That fort can't be anything but a dirt wall. Never in my experience have I heard of — much less seen — regular troops capable of building a complete redoubt in a single night. If regular troops can't do it, these rebel militiamen certainly can't!"

General Howe was correct. No regular troops in the world could prepare a properly fortified redoubt in the few hours that the American militiamen had been laboring on Breed's Hill. But what General Howe and the other British Generals did not know, what they learned only later, was that these New England militiamen were *farmers*. They were farmers who spent their lives digging in the rocky soil of the New World. This life had given them arms of steel. Raw soldiers they may have been (they were actually far more well-trained than the British realized), but when it came to digging and building, no army in the world could do what these men could do with shovels in a single night.

For after Colonel Gridley had marked out the lines of the redoubt the night before, the militiamen had set to digging with a will. Rapidly, the redoubt, one hundred sixty feet long, had begun to take form. By the time the British sentry on the *Lively* first saw it that morning, it was already a formidable defensive position, far stronger than the English officers thought possible.

This, the British Generals did not yet understand. So when Howe laughed at the thought that the militia could have prepared a significant defensive work in the few hours they'd had to work, the other Generals understood the reason for his confidence. Smiling, General Howe continued.

"Besides, that hill has a gentle slope to it. It'll be an easy march for our troops. No militia will stand against our troops marching and firing regular volleys at them. Especially not when they see our lines of bayonets! We'll march our light infantry eastward from Morton's Point around the rebels' left flank, along the shore and *behind* the rebel lines. Then our men will cut back, point south, and attack the Americans from their rear — just as our other formations ascend the hill to the Americans' front. The rebels will panic and break. And surrender." He leaned back with a confident smile.

So the plan was agreed upon. The Generals called for their junior officers, and soon detailed written instructions were sent to the various British regiments that would storm the American positions. The Navy was asked to supply boats in which the soldiers could be rowed across the harbor to the peninsula the Americans had occupied.

Soon the army units in the city of Boston were preparing feverishly for battle. Each infantryman bent himself to polishing his black boots, putting white clay on his broad cartridge belts, preparing for parade-ground perfection of appearance. Packs were loaded with cooked rations, ammunition, clothes — until each man had on his back a weight of more than sixty pounds, with rations for two full days in the field!

Back on Breed's Hill, Colonel Gridley was directing an extension of the American fortifications. He'd looked to the north of the hill, and had seen the gap between the shore and the fence the Americans had fortified.

"That gap along the shore is a path leading right to the rear of our fort," Gridley told his officers. "If the British land troops in Charleston below us," he told them, "they could come around the hill to the north, to our left there, and hit us from the flank and the rear. I want a wall of dirt stretching from the fort down to the river, so we can stop them from doing that. Let's get going!"

Gridley had seen the very possibility upon which the British General Howe had based his plan of action!

Squads of work-hardened farmer-militiamen gathered their shovels and followed Colonel Gridley. Andrew accompanied the Colonel as he directed the digging of the dirt and the building of the wall. The men wielded their shovels with quiet efficiency, and the wall grew before their eyes, one hundred yards long, with a six-foot-high firing platform behind which the militia would be able to shoot at the attacking British soldiers. Periodically, Gridley would send Andrew running with a message to Colonel Prescott, who was directing the work at the redoubt on the hill above.

Justin had remained with Colonel Prescott at the redoubt where the Colonel was driving the men to complete the fortification they'd begun. As the heat of the morning increased, the men began to wilt. But Prescott wouldn't let them stop. "We can't quit now!" he shouted. "You know how the British like to fight: they run at you in long lines with their bayonets. All our men don't have bayonets, so we've got to finish this fort so our men will have something to fight behind. Then we'll cut those redcoats down with our muskets, before they can reach us with their bayonets. Its their lives — or ours — men! Now, dig!"

The men dug.

☆ **CHAPTER SEVEN** ☆

"WE'RE ALMOST OUT OF GUNPOWDER!"

For hours the Americans dug, and built. Soon a wall of dirt stretched from the fort, down the hill, almost to the shore of the river. Now the fort was protected from a British attack that could encircle it from the left and then come back and attack from the rear. On top of Breed's Hill, the redoubt also had a firing platform six feet high behind which the Americans could fire.

As the American officers periodically studied the British formations across the water in Boston, they were astounded at the time it took the English to make ready their attack. Why were they allowing the Americans to finish their fortifications? "What's keeping them?" Prescott asked one of his captains. "It's almost noon, and they've done nothing."

Just then a lookout waved his telescope and yelled: "Their troops are forming in Boston, Colonel."

The officers looked at once across the river. Formations of soldiers were marching to the docks and climbing into small boats. Gangs of sailors were being rowed from the ships in the harbor to man the boats that would carry the soldiers from the Charleston shore. Soon it became apparent that the British planned to ferry their infantrymen across the Harbor to attack the American position.

While the Americans worked furiously to complete their fortifications, Nathan galloped into Charleston with the message from Colonel Prescott. Dashing to General Ward's headquarters, he pulled his horse to a halt, leaned over, and handed Prescott's letter to a sentry standing before headquarters building. Then Nathan wheeled the horse and galloped back across the Charleston Neck toward Breed's Hill. Guns from the British warships were firing at the Neck now, as scattered groups of militiamen marched across in loose formation on their way to Bunker and Breed's Hill. Cannonballs bounded across the ground in front of Nathan's horse as he pounded across. Smoke from the cannons swept across the water. The noise was terrible, and Nathan controlled his mount with great difficulty, gripping the reins in his fist with all his strength.

Behind Breed's Hill, closer to the neck which joined the isthmus to the mainland, General Putnam was feverishly directing the building of fortifications which would provide the Americans with a second line of defense. Twice the veteran officer rode across the narrow neck between the island and the mainland to ask that more gunpowder be sent his troops. The second time he called Andrew to accompany him. As Andrew raced his horse behind the big General, he passed Nathan returning from his mission to Cambridge. Nathan was leaning over his horse's neck, and the animal was stretched out in a desperate run. Cannonballs were bounding along the ground from the British guns, throwing up clouds of dust where they hit, smashing fences and rocks in their path.

"Nathan!" Andrew yelled, as they approached. Nathan looked over, and waved at his friend. He tried to grin. Then

they had swept by each other, Andrew galloping behind the
General, Nathan racing his mount back to Breed's Hill to join
Colonel Prescott. Just as they reached the shore of the mainland, Andrew saw a cannonball skipping along the water
towards them.

"It's going to hit us!" he thought.

But the bouncing iron ball passed just behind their horses'
hooves! And then they were across! Andrew didn't look back
to see where the cannonball had gone. Soon he and General
Putnam had reached the headquarters of General Ward. Here,
men were standing around the front of the building, waiting for
orders. Messengers raced their horses to the fence and leaped
down, shouting as they rushed inside. Others ran out of the
yard, searching for their own mounts. All was bustle and noise.

"General Ward's got fifteen regiments of militia, Andrew,"
Putnam said as they leaped from their horses and hurried into
the building. "He commands the center of the American forces.
But he doesn't see that the men we've got on the Charleston
Peninsula are the only troops actually facing the British!
They've *got* to have more gunpowder if they're going to fight!"

As the angry General Putnam confronted General Ward,
Andrew learned that Ward had reasons for not sending guns
and gunpowder to the men on Bunker and Breed's Hills.

"We're almost out of gunpowder ourselves, General!" General Ward snapped back. "We've only got a few barrels for the
entire army! And we've got to prepare for a British attack on
our right and our left, as well as on Charleston, where you are!
I just can't release any more powder to Bunker Hill!"

"General!" Putnam roared, "we're in firing range of the British right now! Give us cannons that will reach their ships and we'll force them to evacuate Boston! Give us gunpowder for our muskets so our men can defend themselves! The British are about to attack us and we've got to have the powder and bullets to shoot them down before they reach our militia with their bayonets! You know what those bayonets will do to our militia who don't have them!"

General Ward refused to budge. "We just can't spare any more, Putnam," he snapped. "There's not enough for our regiments here in Cambridge. We've got to have powder and bullets here."

Then General Ward's advisors called him into another room. Putnam and Andrew waited impatiently. After a while, General Ward came back.

"We'll send you the New Hampshire regiments under Colonel Stark," he said. "They'll support your forces on the Charleston Peninsula.

Without a word General Putnam snapped, "Let's go, Andrew." The two rushed from the room, Putnam in a rage. They ran out the door and leaped to their saddles. "I'm glad to have the New Hampshire regiments," Putnam said to Andrew, "but if we don't get more powder and bullets to the forces we have, they won't do us much good."

He wheeled his horse to leave, then turned back to Andrew and pointed to his right where a long line of men stood at ease. "That's Stark over there, Andrew," he said, "in front of his men. General Ward's aide is taking him his order now. Go over and introduce yourself, and tell him you'll lead him to me at

the fort on Breed's Hill. I'll get back right away!" Wheeling
his mount quickly, Putnam galloped off.

"Yes, sir," Andrew replied, turning his horse and riding over
to Colonel Stark. The Colonel welcomed him with a tight smile,
and told him to stick with him. "We've just been given some
powder, Andrew," he explained, "but we don't have bullets.
My men are melting down lead from the pipes of a church organ
in Cambridge — that'll give us something to shoot from our
rifles."

Andrew was appalled at the prospect facing these American
militia. How could they fight the British troops — the finest
army in the world! — without sufficient powder and proper
bullets for their muskets and rifles? For the New Hampshire
men, he learned, were riflemen — almost as deadly with their
long rifles as Virginians. They could really shoot, and they
could bring down enemy soldiers at a distance — if they had
powder and bullets!

"You mean, your men don't have proper bullets?" he asked
Colonel Stark incredulously.

"That's right, Andrew," the Colonel replied. "We've fired
all ours in practice. We were told we'd be given more when we
arrived, but now they say that they don't have enough themselves."

"Then what will you do, sir?" the Virginian asked, stunned.

"We'll do the best we can, boy," Stark replied. "We'll shoot
as long as we can. We can do no more."

Just then a man rushed up to the Colonel. "We've given out the powder and bullets, Colonel. Each man has fifteen shots apiece. That's all — there's no more!"

"We'll do what we can with it," the Colonel repeated grimly. "Form up the men. We'll march at once."

As the marching formations reached the narrow piece of land between the Mystic River and Boston Harbor, they saw the British warships firing at the Americans who dared to cross over to Charleston. Groups of militiamen ran across the Neck, hoping to escape the British shot. The dangerous low ground provided no cover at all from the British cannons.

Andrew never forgot that march across the bullet-swept Charleston Neck to the American fortifications on Breed's Hill. The roar of the cannons and the plunging shot threw his horse almost into a panic and the boy had to grip the reins with all his strength to keep the terrified animal under control. He wanted desperately to put the horse into a furious gallop so he could cross the narrow spit of land as soon as possible and get out of range of those British cannon. But he knew he couldn't give in to his fears; the New Hampshire men were marching with deliberate order, and he had to keep his horse to a walk beside their leader.

Now the British cannon balls were striking the ground all around the men, bouncing and skipping across the shallow piece of land that connected the isthmus with the mainland.

One of Stark's officers spoke up. "We'd better run the men across, Colonel! Those ships' guns are getting the range!"

"One fresh man in action is worth ten tired ones," Stark replied calmly, refusing to increase his pace. Stark would not tire his men by running them across the Neck. So the militia continued their steady deliberate march as the men tried hard to ignore the British cannons. Behind them marched another regiment of New Hampshire militia under Colonel Reed.

Now the British were firing cannons from all of their ships in the Harbor and in the river. In addition to their warships, the British also had barges with cannons anchored in the river and the bay, and guns from these were firing furiously against the American fortifications. The ceaseless roar of the big guns became nerve-racking to the American militia, many of whom had never heard such a cannonade, let alone been the object of it. At the redoubt, Andrew saw the American officers speak to calm their men under the British fire. Fortunately, many of the cannonballs were falling short of the fort. But some were still rolling a long way when they hit the ground, and these knocked down men who failed to get out of their path.

Smoke from the firing ships and batteries drifted across the water. Shouts and orders from the warships sometimes reached the ears of the Americans on shore. Then, from Boston across the harbor, came the dreaded sounds of British army fifes and drums. The Americans on the hills of the Charleston peninsula turned their heads toward the city, and saw the sunlight flash off the rifles of British infantry units marching to the docks.

The British were preparing to board their soldiers on boats and row them across the water to the town of Charleston. From there they would march to attack the American lines.

On Breed's Hill, Colonel Stark and his officers had gathered to confer with Colonel Prescott. Here the officers stood and gazed somberly at the town below them, the town toward which the British boats were now rowing. "They're coming across!" Stark said calmly. "They're putting their infantrymen in small boats, and rowing them across to the town."

Across the narrow causeway swept by the British naval guns, Andrew rode beside Colonel Stark as he led his riflemen past Bunker Hill. "There's the general, sir," Andrew said to Stark, pointing out General Putnam who had just galloped his horse down the hill toward the New Hampshire militiamen.

Soon Colonel Stark had joined the other officers at the redoubt. Silently, they watched the British units on the docks across the river.

At one o'clock the British were ready to attack. Looking down from the hills above, the colonial militiamen watched in silence as the redcoated regiments began to move, their long bayonet-tipped muskets held before them in deadly lines.

CHAPTER EIGHT

BRITISH SPIES!

Sarah Edwards and Rachel Hendricks walked quickly along the walk, violins under their arms. The town was filled with militiamen whose drummers beat martial airs as the various militia groups marched in formation through the streets.

"Goodness!" Rachel said, her brown eyes wide with excitement, "I bet Andrew and Nathan would wish they were here now!"

"I bet they would!" Sarah agreed. "All they wanted was to get close to the marching men, and here in Williamsburg they'd have their wish every day!"

"I wonder what they're doing now," Rachel asked, as they stepped around a group of older men standing and talking on the walk.

"They're probably just sitting in that old warehouse in New York, counting barrels of cargo," Sarah replied.

Sarah was almost thirteen, a year older than Rachel. She wore a deep blue dress with white trim, and a white collar which framed her long dark hair. Rachel was dressed in a dark green dress, which accentuated her light brown hair and brown eyes. The two girls were on their way to their weekly violin lesson from Mrs. Gardiner, a matron who taught numbers of Williamsburg citizens violin and harpsichord. Her husband was a merchant in town, whose business took him often to Yorktown.

The girls came to their teacher's house, a neat, two-story green home surrounded by a white picket fence. Letting themselves through the gate, they walked up the three steps to the porch. Sarah lifted the big brass knocker and let it fall.

Mrs. Gardiner, a portly lady in blue, with round red face and gray hair, threw open the door with a smile. "Come in, girls!" she said. "I've been expecting you!"

Sarah and Rachel went into the hall of the lovely home as Mrs. Gardiner closed the door and led them to the music room.

"Where's Andrew?" she asked Rachel, as the girls got out their music and put this on the stands.

"He and Nathan are in New York, Mrs. Gardiner," Rachel replied. "He'll miss some lessons, I'm afraid."

"New York?" she asked, raising her eyebrows. "Isn't that close to Boston? And the British army?"

"Well, not really," Rachel answered. "Its a long way south of Boston. They're not going close to Boston."

"What are they doing in New York at a time like this?" Mrs. Gardiner asked as she took up her own violin.

"Our fathers sent them on the *Morning Star* with a load of cargo," Sarah answered. "They'll be back in several weeks. And I know Andrew will have his music ready."

"Well, I have no worry about that," the genial lady replied. "He's really quite talented, and very serious about his practicing, I know. Now, let's see how serious you two were about *your* practicing this past week! Let's play the Vivaldi first."

The half-hour passed rapidly for the girls. They loved playing their instruments, and they loved the friendly lady who was nevertheless a very demanding teacher. The lesson was over all too quickly, and the girls gathered up their violins and their music.

Just then there was a loud knock on the door. "That'll be Stephen," Mrs. Gardiner said.

Sarah and Rachel noticed that she was not smiling. They'd known how difficult these times had been on everyone in Williamsburg. People were divided over the matter of resistance to Great Britain. Old friends argued with each other, and many friendships had been severed. But they had become puzzled at Mrs. Gardiner's attitude toward Stephen Bancroft, a seventeen year old boy who'd been taking lessons as long as they had. The girls didn't particularly care for him, but they had no reason to dislike him either. Yet it had become obvious to them that Mrs. Gardiner was not pleased when he came.

"Stephen's father's a patriot, isn't he?" Sarah asked.

Mrs. Gardiner didn't reply at once. She looked steadily at Sarah without speaking for a long moment. Then she replied. "As you know, girls, my husband and I are patriots too. But I'm not letting these matters interfere with my friendships! I'm teaching patriots and I'm teaching those whose families want to remain loyal to Great Britain. I hope all this trouble will blow over so that everyone can be friends again!"

"Yes, ma'am," Sarah said. "But Papa says that people are really mad that the Governor took his family to live on the British ship. He won't come back to meet the members of the legislature. That's made it hard for people to think that everyone can get along, he thinks."

"Your Papa's right, Sarah," Mrs. Gardiner replied with a troubled frown. Then her face seemed to become almost grim. "I'll go let Stephen in," she said, as she left the room.

"Why is she acting so strange about Stephen?" Rachel asked Sarah quietly. "And she didn't answer your question when you asked if Stephen's family were patriots."

"I don't know why she's acting so strange about him," Sarah replied, blue eyes troubled. "And you're right — she didn't answer my question. She's acted funny about him for several weeks, hasn't she? She must know something that troubles her."

"I'm not sure I trust him," Rachel said.

"Neither am I," Sarah agreed.

Stephen came in then, violin under his arm. A broad smile lit his face as he saw the two girls. He was a big young man, tall, with broad shoulders and blond hair. He was expensively dressed, as usual, and cut a fine figure in his long coat. Sarah thought his smile was not quite sincere, but she and Rachel were always polite to him. Each week the two girls tried to leave Mrs. Gardiner's house as soon as their lesson was over and before the boy arrived, but he'd always come right on time.

"Hello!" he said genially, staring first at Rachel, then at Sarah. The two girls replied politely, they hurried to the door which Mrs. Gardiner was holding open for them.

Just then, a young man in expensive clothes ran up to the steps and asked Mrs. Gardiner if he could speak to Stephen before he began his lesson. The music teacher told Rachel and Sarah goodbye, then went back into the house and called Stephen to the door. The young man waited outside on the porch.

When Rachel stepped out the door she turned to her right to avoid the young man, and stumbled. The loose pages of music fell from her hands and fluttered to the porch to the right of the doorway, several feet away from the door. The young man had stepped just inside the door, and was so intent on seeing Stephen that he didn't notice this, nor offer to help her pick up the scattered papers.

Rachel's face was red with embarrassment as she knelt quickly in confusion and began to gather the pages. Sarah knelt beside her and helped pick them up. Thus they heard Stephen come to the door and speak to the young man. But Stephen too remained inside, so that both boys were out of their sight. The boys thus had no way of knowing that Rachel and Sarah were on the porch close by, and could hear every word that they said.

"Here's the message!" the young man said to Stephen in a whisper. "Father says you're to get this to the Governor right away!" He pulled a letter from his pocket and handed it to Stephen.

"All right," Stephen whispered back, taking the letter and jamming it into the pages of music he was holding. "Those despicable rebels don't know what they're in for — thinking they can make war against the King!"

Sarah and Rachel, kneeling close together, looked at each other with shock in their eyes. So Stephen and his family were *not* patriots after all! And they were getting information to the Governor! And this young man was a messenger for the Governor's friends! The girls' backs were to the door, and they kept their heads down as they quietly gathered up the loose pages of music.

I hope they don't come out on the porch and see us! Sarah thought to herself. Rachel was thinking the same thing.

The messenger spoke again, in a quiet voice. "This letter gives a list of the militia companies that Virginia is mobilizing, and tells about the state of their weapons."

"I bet it's pretty pitiful!" Stephen snorted derisively.

"Well, they don't have many cannons, but they have a lot of armed men," the messenger said.

"It won't matter how many armed men they have, " Stephen replied with a snarl, "not when the British regiments land! England has the best army in the world!"

"They can't get here too soon for me!" the messenger whispered bitterly. "Those rebels have got to be taught a lesson!"

"I've got to go," Stephen whispered quickly. "Mrs. Gardiner's waiting. Thanks. My father will get these to the Governor tonight."

"How will he do it?" the messenger asked.

"He'll send a man down river to a small boat. The Governor's got men waiting there for messengers. They'll take it out to the *Fowey* — that's the warship he and his family are on. He'll know what to do with this!"

"Did you see that the Gazette published the Governor's letter to London, where he asked for a blockade by British ships to stop all shipping from entering and leaving Virginia!"

"Yes. And that's made the Virginians mad as hornets! 'Bye!" Stephen turned then, and hurried back into the house.

The messenger wheeled around, rushed out the door without closing it, and ran quickly down the steps. Dashing through the gate he hurriedly untied his horse's reins from the rail and leaped into the saddle. Sarah and Rachel wondered anxiously if he'd still see them through the porch railing, but he wheeled the horse around and never looked back. Kicking the animal into motion, he galloped away.

As the horse pounded down the street the two girls leaped up, violins and pages of music clutched in their hands, and hurried down the steps and through the gate.

"Stephen's a British spy!" Sarah exclaimed in a shocked whisper as the two turned and began hurrying home.

"He sure is!" Rachel replied. "And so is his father! But everyone thinks that they're patriots!"

"My goodness, I wonder how much information they've already given to the Governor?" Sarah asked, eyes wide at this revelation of treachery in the patriot ranks.

"We've got to tell our fathers right away!" Rachel said.

"It's a good thing that messenger didn't see us on the porch!" Sarah said. "I wonder what Stephen would have done if they'd found us overhearing their conversation?"

"Well, they can't do anything to us for picking up our music!" Rachel said indignantly. "This isn't England — it's Virginia!"

"Still, I wonder what they might have done," Sarah said again. "They wouldn't want this information to get back to our fathers — everyone *knows* that our families are patriots. I bet they would have tried to stop us from getting home somehow."

"Goodness" exclaimed Rachel, eyes wide at the thought. "Are things really that bad, Sarah?"

"Well, there's fighting in Massachusetts already. And a patriot army surrounds Boston, blocking the British inside the city. I think anything can happen when men know that they're at war."

As the two girls hastened along Francis Street they were suddenly startled by a shout behind them.

"Don't look!" Sarah said at once. "I know that's Jed! I recognize his voice!"

"I couldn't help it!" Rachel replied, turning back, a worried frown on her face. "And it *is* Jed — that troublemaker! He's calling us."

"He can call us all he wants," Sarah said emphatically, "but it won't do him any good."

"Andrew said he'd beat Jed up if he bothered us again," Rachel reminded her friend as they hurried along the dusty walkway beside the picket fences that fronted the houses.

"Nathan would too, but I hope it doesn't come to that," Sarah said anxiously. "Jed's a lot bigger than either of them."

"His size wouldn't matter," Rachel said confidently. "Those boys know how to fight."

"Well, our fathers would certainly see that he stays away from us if we have to tell them," Sarah said. "We don't want our brothers getting hurt."

Jed shouted again. His voice sounded closer now.

"I bet he knows that Andrew and Nathan are gone," Rachel said. "He wouldn't bother us if he thought that they were here."

"He won't bother us now," Sarah said.

She was wrong. They heard the sound of running steps behind them, and then a big young man wearing baggy brown pants and loose white shirt ran up and wheeled to stand before them, blocking their way. The two girls halted before him.

CHAPTER NINE

"RIDE FAST, GIRLS!"

"Hey, can't you girls speak to a man?" Jed asked with a leer.

Tall, thick-set, with powerful shoulders and arms, he stood solidly before them, hands on hips. His once-white shirt was streaked with dirt, his loose brown pants were dirty and unkempt. He had a wide face, small gray eyes, and thick dark hair. Jed Marks was known to be a bully.

Without a word the two girls separated and simply walked around him.

"Hey!" he said, shocked at their move. Turning, he ran to catch up, and again planted himself directly in front of them. They came to a halt. His smile was gone now, and his eyes had turned ugly.

"You girls are pretty stuck up if you can't even talk," he said. Anger made his red face even redder, they saw.

"You'd better leave us alone, or we'll tell our fathers," Sarah replied quietly. Her heart was beating quickly, but she wasn't going to let this boy stop them.

Jed blinked at this. "Tell your fathers what?" he asked. "That a man spoke polite-like to you, and you was too rude to answer?"

"Tell our fathers that you stood in our way when we wanted to go home!" Sarah replied quietly. "Let us by!"

Jed blinked again. Then he mustered a smirk on his large red face. "Aw, now," he said, "I wouldn't want your fathers to be bothered by alarms from a couple of skeerdy girls. Go ahead! Go on home!" He stepped aside and made a mocking bow.

The girls walked by. He laughed at them as they passed. Then, as they walked away from him, the smile vanished from his face. "Some of you patriots will be surprised when the British fleet brings a British army to Virginia," he said. "Then you'll be a bit more polite to a man, I think."

They said not a word to this. This angered him even more. But he wasn't about to do anything that would bring the girls' fathers' wrath on him. Turning angrily, he stalked away.

Sarah and Rachel crossed the street then, and hurried along for another block before turning to the right. "So he's for the British too!" Rachel said. "Not so long ago, we heard that he was a patriot. Goodness, Sarah — how many people in town think like he does?"

"Lots of people, Papa says," Sarah answered. "They change when the news changes. When they think the patriots are strong, they're patriots. When they think we'll all bow down to the King, they switch to his side. Some of them do, at least. But not all are like Jed. Most of the people loyal to the King are good citizens like our families, Papa says — they just see things differently than we do. They think we shouldn't do anything to anger Great Britain. Some of them say we have no right to oppose England. Others say it's just foolish to think the colonies could possibly win a fight with the British Empire."

"Do you think that they're right?" Rachel asked.

"I don't know!" Sarah replied. "Papa says it won't be easy. But he says that the way the British treat their enemies is awful — and the King has declared Massachusetts an enemy. And Parliament has said they can rule us in everything, absolutely everything! And Governor Dunmore has asked the King to declare Virginia an enemy, and he's asked for fleets and armies to be sent here to conquer us. That would be awful, Papa says, and that's why we don't have any choice but to defend ourselves against their armies. Oh, it's terrible, Rachel!"

Soon the girls were home. Passing Sarah's house, they rushed to Rachel's home next door, where they expected to find their fathers. Hurriedly the two ran up the steps of the porch and rushed inside. Carolyn Hendricks, Rachel's mother, was in the kitchen, putting fresh bread on the table when the girls burst in and startled her.

"Where's Father?" Rachel cried.

"Goodness, Rachel," Carolyn Hendricks replied, wiping her face with her apron, "what's the matter? You two look as if the devil were after you!"

"Maybe he is, Mrs. Hendricks," Sarah replied. "That Jed bothered us again as we came home. And Stephen Bancroft is a British spy!"

"Stephen? Where did you see him?"

Breathlessly the two girls told her of the conversation they'd overheard between Stephen and the messenger. "Stephen's father is sending information to Governor Dunmore!" Rachel concluded.

"My goodness!" Carolyn Hendricks said, shocked. "We all thought that Stephen's family were patriots!"

"But they're not!" Sarah answered. "They despise the patriots. We heard them talk!"

"Your two fathers are in their office right now. Go tell them what you heard," Carolyn Hendricks said quickly.

Rachel and Sarah rushed out of the house and down the steps of the porch. Running to the gate, they dashed through this, then ran to the one story office their fathers used for their business. This had its own front entrance, and toward this the two girls ran. Behind the office were outbuildings, the barn, and a large shed for storing the barrels of foodstuffs their firm shipped regularly to the northern colonies.

The girls rushed into the office and found both their fathers busy working. But the men dropped their business at once and listened intently to the story Sarah and Rachel told them. When the girls had finished, William Hendricks asked the first question.

"When will Stephen take the letter to the boat that'll take it to the Governor?"

Sarah and Rachel looked at each other. "Tonight," Rachel replied. "Stephen said 'tonight'. He didn't mention an hour." Sarah nodded agreement.

"Then we've got to get word to the committee right away," Nelson Edwards said quickly. "They'll have to assign someone to watch Stephen's house and intercept that letter when he leaves the house."

"Maybe it would be better if they grabbed Stephen before he got that message back to his father," William Hendricks suggested. "That'll also scare them — and maybe stop that source of information for the Governor, for a while at least."

Nelson Edwards pondered this. "I think you're right, William," he said finally. "In that case, let's send the girls to Captain Innes at once, with a note telling what they've overheard. That way, he can act as soon as he wishes — or wait if he wants to. Girls, run out and tell Wilbur to saddle the horses for you. You'll have to ride if Captain Innes is to get this in time to intercept Stephen."

The girls ran into the back of the store and found Wilbur, one of their fathers' hired hands. A giant of a man, with thick blond hair, he was rolling barrels from a storeroom to a back door. Outside, a large freight wagon was being loaded.

"Wilbur!" Sarah said breathlessly, "father says for you to please saddle *Belle* and *Princess* right away! We've got to ride to Captain Innes at once!"

"Sure," the big man smiled, stacking the barrel against the wall, and stepping rapidly out the back door. "I'll have 'em ready in a minute."

Sarah and Rachel thanked him, then turned and rushed back into the office. Nelson Edwards was seated at his desk, hastily writing. William Hendricks stood beside him, and the two consulted in quiet tones as Edwards composed the message. The girls stood just inside the door and waited.

The windows were open and light poured into the room. The girls heard birds singing in nearby trees, and the sounds of men putting barrels into a wagon behind the office.

"Goodness," Sarah said quietly to Rachel, "we didn't know we'd be getting so deep into things!" Her blue eyes were wide at the thought.

"What if I hadn't dropped those pages of music?" Rachel asked. "Then we wouldn't even know that Stephen and his family were helping the British!"

"I'm still wondering what would have happened if that man and Stephen had seen us on the porch," Sarah said. "I know they wouldn't have wanted to let us go straight home — not without questioning us, at least, to find out if we'd understood their conversation!"

Then their fathers called them, and the girls turned to reply.

"Take this note to Captain Innes right away!" Nelson Edwards said, handing a folded paper to Sarah. "He's meeting with some men at Bruton Parish Church, and he'll be in the churchyard. Just go up to him and hand this to him. Tell him we sent you, and that it's urgent that he read this at once. Then answer any questions he asks — and come straight back!"

"Understand that, girls?" William Hendricks said emphatically. "The town's filled with a lot of militiamen right now, and we don't want you girls to be bothered by them."

"Yes, sir," the girls replied.

"Tell Captain Innes when this happened," Nelson Edwards added, "and that he'll have to act fast if he decides to grab

Stephen before he gets home and hands that note to his father. But don't mention Stephen's name — or anything about this letter - to anyone but the captain. We don't want to start a round of gossip!"

"Yes, father," Sarah replied.

"Ride fast, Girls!" William Hendricks said quietly.

Sarah and Rachel turned and rushed out the door. Wilbur and another man had just thrown saddles on the girls' horses, and were tightening the cinches. Wilbur held the reins of Sarah's brown mare, *Belle*, and the other man held Rachel's gray, whose name was *Princess*.

"They're ready, girls," Wilbur smiled. "But don't let them get spooked in the street — there's too many riders dashing around these days, all of them going as fast as their horses will fly, it seems!"

"We'll be careful, Wilbur," Sarah smiled, as she approached *Belle*. Wilbur stooped and cupped his big hands for her foot. She stepped into his hands, and he lifted her up. Settling herself easily in the side-saddle, she took the reins Wilbur handed her. Her wide blue skirts reached down past her feet and stirrups. Wilbur helped Rachel mount then, and when Sarah looked over she saw that Rachel was ready to ride, her eyes shining with excitement.

Waving their thanks to the two men, the girls walked their horses toward the back gate, past two wagons that were in process of being loaded. At the gate they turned, saw that there were no horses or wagons in their way, and put their horses into a run.

"Will we reach Captain Innes in time for him to capture Stephen?" Rachel called as the two horses ran side by side down the street.

"I hope so!" Sarah called back over the sound of the galloping hooves.

They turned left on Francis Street and slowed their pace. Two large freight wagons were heading their way, and the girls didn't want their own horses spooked by the animals that were drawing the wagons. When they'd trotted carefully past the big wagons, Sarah and Rachel put their horses into a run once more. A flock of chickens scattered before them as they reached the next corner and a cloud of dust rose in the air behind them.

Here they turned right, and galloped their mounts again.

They came to the broad Duke of Gloucester Street, and swept into the broad lane toward Bruton Parish Church.

CHAPTER TEN

"BRING HIM BACK, AT ONCE!"

When Sarah and Rachel reached the Palace Green, they turned toward the Governor's Palace, pulled their horses to a stop, and dismounted. To their right they saw a squad of militia men marching down the broad Green toward the Palace. Hastily the girls tied their horses' reins to the rail just outside the brick wall that surrounded Bruton Parish Church. Then they hurried through the iron gate and into the churchyard. Walking quickly along the length of the tall brick building they turned to their left and found themselves at the main entrance of the church. Here they found a crowd of armed men standing around Captain Innes. The captain was speaking.

The girls came to the edge of the gathering, and hesitated, uncertain about interrupting the captain. But one of the men at the back of the gathering heard them walk up, turned around, and recognized them at once.

"Sarah, Rachel, what are you two doing here?" he asked with a friendly smile. A short, stout man, he wore the customary knee breeches with white stockings, and a brown coat. His tricorn hat sat high on his head and he smiled genially at the two girls.

"Oh, Mr. Greene," Sarah said, "we've got an urgent message for Captain Innes from our fathers!"

"Certainly," Mr. Greene said, his face becoming serious at this news, "just follow me." Turning, he pushed his way through the men. The girls followed close behind as the men moved to let them through. Mr. Greene walked right up to Captain Innes.

"Captain," he said quietly, "these are William Hendrick's and Nelson Edwards' girls, and their fathers have sent you an urgent message."

Sarah and Rachel were suddenly embarrassed to find themselves in the midst of the group of men who had parted to let them through, and now stood staring curiously at them. But Captain Innes smiled reassuringly, and beckoned to them, so they approached. Sarah handed him the letter, and he took this now with a puzzled frown, opened it, and began to read. The men around him had backed away a bit, wondering what could be so important as to bring two young girls to interrupt the meeting of the town's militia. But Captain Innes' face grew grim as he studied the letter. When he finished reading he glanced up, looking sharply at Sarah and Rachel.

"Can you lead us to this young man now?" he asked.

"Yes, Sir," Sarah said, "I believe we can. He'll walk home after his lesson, and we know the way he takes."

"Ben!" Captain Innes said decisively, turning and addressing a big man who stood beside him. "Read this!"

The Captain handed him the letter and waited impatiently for him to read it. Ben was tall, large in every way, and deeply tanned. He was dressed in a hunting shirt and dark trousers which were tucked into brightly polished leather boots. On his head he wore the popular black tricorn hat.

Ben read the letter quickly, then looked up, anger on his face. "James, what do you want me to do? I'm not sure I know this man."

"These girls do," Captain Innes replied. "Pick out five men and follow them — they know the way he'll be coming. Bring him back here to me. I'll dismiss these men in a moment, so we can question him privately. Don't arrest him officially — just bring him back! At once!"

"Yes, sir," Ben said eagerly. He looked up at the assembled men and picked out five men, calling them by name. They stepped forward, rifles in hand.

"Let's go, boys, we've got a chore!" Ben announced quietly, as he turned and headed along the walk toward the hitch rail where the girls had just tied their own horses.

Captain Innes spoke quietly to Sarah and Rachel. "Girls, I'd be obliged if you'd be willing to ride with Ben and identify this young man to him."

Sarah and Rachel, awed at the responsibility, conscious that all the men were looking at them, agreed to do this.

"I hope Ben can catch him before he gets home," Captain Innes continued. "If he does, you girls go back and thank your fathers for me. And accept my thanks as well. If Ben can't catch this man before he gets to his house, please come back here and tell us all you know about this. We'll try to get him later." His serious face broke into a warm smile then, and he added, "You girls have done us a great service. Thank you!"

"Yes, sir," they replied, blushing at his words of praise. The two were quite conscious of the curious stares of the assembled men as they turned to go out to their horses. The men who'd clustered around again to listen moved out of their way, and Sarah and Rachel filed through their ranks, back to the gate that led to the Palace Green and the hitching rail where their horses were tied.

When the girls stepped through the gate, Ben and three of his men had already untied their horses and swung into their saddles. The girls rushed to the hitch rail. Here they found that Ben had stationed a man at each of their horses to help them mount. The men cupped their hands for the girls' feet, helped them up, then ran to their own steeds and vaulted into their saddles.

"Ride with me, girls!" Ben called. The horsemen parted to let Sarah and Rachel ride up beside Ben as he led the group at a trot toward Duke of Gloucester Street just a few yards away.

Sarah rode up to Ben's right, Rachel to his left, and as the group reached the broad street he asked them, "Which way?"

"That way," Sarah pointed. She quickly explained where their music teacher lived, and the street Stephen would take to walk home when he'd finished his lesson. She told him what time Stephen had come, and when he usually left.

"We may still be in time to catch him," Ben said. He turned back to his men. "We're going to intercept a man, then bring him back to the Captain. Let's ride!" He kicked his horse into a run, and the girls did the same.

The group broke into a gallop down the broad street, scattering a flock of wildly squawking chickens. People walking in the dusty road heard the pounding hooves and moved out of their way. A pack of small dogs broke out barking, ran with them for a short way, then gave up. Dust swirled from the flashing hooves of the horses, sparks flew up when they hit rocks, and the girls concentrated on keeping their saddles at the head of the galloping cavalcade.

People on the side of the street and in front of the stores turned to look at the band of riders with two young girls in their sidesaddles riding like the wind beside the leader. A flock of pigeons rose into the air in front of Rachel's horse, and for a frantic moment she thought that *Princess* would balk and throw her. Gripping the reins with all her strength she held the mount on course.

Then they came to the corner. Ben, flanked by Sarah and Rachel, led the other riders in a wide turn without slacking speed. Sarah and Rachel were excellent riders, but they weren't used to riding at the head of a group of armed men, and they rode with fierce concentration, praying desperately that they'd be able to keep up with the leader.

Oh, I hope that we're in time! Sarah thought to herself.

When they came to the next street, Ben called a halt, and the cavalcade pulled up in a swirl of dust. "Which way will he be coming from?" he asked the girls, as the excited animals danced in agitation.

"That way," Sarah pointed down the street to her right. "When he finishes his lesson, he'll come from there."

"All right," Ben said. "You girls ride forward with me. When you see him, just point him out. Then you move out of the way so my men can join me. And then I want you to ride away — get out of sight so Stephen doesn't see you!"

"Yes, sir," the girls replied.

Ben told the other riders the plan, then led the group in a slow walk down the street, with Sarah and Rachel flanking him on either side. The cavalcade had passed only a few houses when suddenly Rachel spotted Stephen walking toward them just half a block ahead.

"There he is!" she said to Ben, as she pointed ahead.

"You sure?" Ben asked. His face was stern now, his jaw set, as his gray eyes spotted the man Rachel had indicated.

"Yes, sir," Rachel answered.

"That's him," Sarah added. "That's Stephen!"

"Let my men through, girls!" Ben said. "Go back home — and thanks! You've done a great service for Virginia!"

Sarah and Rachel pulled their mounts away from Ben as the five men behind them came up quickly and closed with their leader. The men began walking their horses toward the approaching young man. The girls turned and put their horses into a trot, heading in the opposite direction. When they'd covered about fifty yards, Sarah and Rachel pulled to a stop, and looked back. Their horses stamped restlessly and pranced, still excited, and difficult to hold.

Stephen stood by a white picket fence, surrounded by the six riders. He appeared to be arguing with them. Then the girls saw him mount behind one of the men. The group of horsemen wheeled, and rode back toward the girls on their way to Bruton Parish Church.

"Let's go," Sarah said quickly, "before he recognizes us!"

She wheeled *Belle*, Rachel turned *Princess*, and the two galloped back down the street followed by a cloud of dust thrown up by their horses' hooves. The pair swept around the corner to the right, and ran their mounts along the road between the rows of houses. Half-way down that block, Sarah slowed *Belle* to a walk. Rachel did the same. The horses pranced and tossed their heads, then settled down.

"Goodness!" Rachel exclaimed. "That was so close — he was almost home!" Her cap had been blown off her head by the breeze, but she hadn't noticed.

"He almost got way!" Sarah agreed. "Now, Captain Innes and the patriots will see the message he's carrying before he can give it to his father. Then the Governor won't get it! Imagine," she exclaimed, eyes wide at the enormity of the thought, "Stephen and his father planned to tell the British Governor about all Virginia's militia companies!"

"And the Governor wants the King to blockade us just like they're blockading Boston!" Rachel replied. "Does that mean that England has declared war against us?"

"Father says that it does," Sarah replied. "That's why all the colonists have to unite to defend themselves, he says. Because the King and the Parliament have already declared that the Colonies are in rebellion, so they're sending their armies to take away our weapons and munitions."

Sobered by the reality of the impending war, the girls fell silent. Then Sarah reminded her friend of the need of haste. "We'd better hurry back home and tell our fathers what's happened."

They put their horses into a trot.

Behind them, Ben and his men, with Stephen their prisoner, rode back toward Bruton Parish Church. Suddenly, a young man stepped from behind a large tree as the group of horsemen passed by him, stared hard at the mounted men and their prisoner, and swore. He was the same man who'd brought the message to Stephen as he went for his violin lesson. He'd seen the two girls lead the men toward Stephen — he'd recognized them, in fact, although they hadn't seen him hiding behind a tree as they'd passed. He'd seen them identify Stephen to the militiamen. And he'd seen Stephen captured and led away.

Now, watching Stephen taken away, he realized the damage those two girls had done to the Governor's cause. *Those are the girls Jed Marks pointed out to me*, he thought to himself. *They're the same girls who sent the message to warn Patrick Henry about the Governor's plan to arrest him. Why, they're nothing but Patriot spies!*

He turned and walked quickly in the direction that Ben and his riders had taken. The horsemen had already turned and were out of sight. Resisting the urge to break into a run, he continued his rapid course until he came to the corner. Then he turned in the opposite direction from Ben and his men, and hurried home, his mind in a turmoil, his face twisted with anger at the thought of Sarah and Rachel leading the militia to capture Stephen.

Father's got to tell the Governor about these girls! he thought to himself. *Something's got to be done to stop their spying.*

Then he had another thought: *Maybe our men should kidnap one of them and take her to the Governor's ship!*

CHAPTER ELEVEN

"THE REDCOATS ARE ABOUT TO ATTACK!"

With chilled hearts, Andrew, Nathan, and Justin stood on Breed's Hill with a crowd of militiamen and stared across the waters to Boston where long ranks of English soldiers marched through the streets and approached the wharves.

With fifes blowing and drums beating their stirring tunes the ominous red-coated columns marched with full field packs down to the waterfront. Halting at the docks, the troops began to file into the waiting boats. Sailors from the fleet held their oars as the heavily laden infantrymen clambered awkwardly into the rocking small vessels and packed themselves tightly together on the broad wooden seats. The soldiers were dangerously — foolishly over-loaded. They bore full field packs which carried three days' rations for each man, heavy uniform coats, the massive deadly "Brown Bess" muskets, and the decisive infantry weapon of the age — the gleaming steel bayonets. Never happy on the water, the infantrymen packed themselves nervously like sardines into the deeply laden boats, waiting to be ferried to battle.

Then the boats pushed off from the docks, and the sailors began to pull their heavy loads across the water to the village of Charleston, just opposite Boston. And now the cannonade from the British ships and forts increased in fury. Again and again the air was shattered by thunderous volleys of the heavy guns. Smoke poured unceasingly from the sides of the warships, from the floating batteries moored off-shore, and from batteries around Boston itself.

The American militiamen on Breed's Hill watched fascinated as slowly, inexorably, the infantry-laden boats were rowed across the water, headed for Charleston Point. Here they were out of range of the American fort on Breed's Hill, and here General Howe figured they would make an unopposed landing. Once on shore, the units would be formed, and the attack would begin.

High atop Breed's Hill, Colonel Prescott watched the British troops debark from the ships and fan out on Moulton's Point before the village of Charleston. "They're spreading to our left," he said to his officers. "We've got to extend our lines down that hill, or they'll come around our left flank and surround us."

Quickly Prescott strode over to where Andrew and Nathan stood with several militiamen observing the British deployment. "Amos," he called, singling out a young militiaman from the formation in front of him. "Come here." The young man trotted quickly to obey, a heavy rifle cradled easily in his arm.

Prescott turned and spotted Andrew and Nathan. He waved them to him. "This is Amos Burns," the Colonel said, introducing the militiaman to the two Virginians. Andrew and Nathan shook hands with Amos, a stocky young farmer in brown homespun trousers and shirt, with the typical broad-brimmed hat of the militiamen. They noted that the young man seemed very much at home with the long rifle he now held in his hand.

"I want you to go with him to Colonel Stark," Colonel Prescott told them. "Tell him the British are deploying to our left — in his front — and that I'm sending men to extend our fortifications down the hill to cover his right. I think they'll try to hit his unit and turn our flank."

"Yes, sir," the young men replied.

Prescott continued. "Ask Colonel Stark to keep me abreast of any British movements in his front. Tell him to let me know if he needs help."

Then Colonel Prescott suddenly remembered the late-night discussion with Jeremiah Hanson, when Putnam had first requested that the boys be used as messengers for his army. Hanson had agreed that they could serve as messengers, but had made it plain that he had no authority to commit them to combat, and that they should not be so employed.

"I just remembered, boys," the Colonel said, "you were loaned to us as messengers — not soldiers. I have no right to involve you in the fighting. You may leave at once, and ride across the Neck back to Cambridge. And thank you for all you've done."

Andrew and Nathan looked at each other. They knew that their fathers had not expected them to come this close to the American army. They knew that John Turnbull had loaned them to Mr. Brown only to help with the shipment of gunpowder to the army in Cambridge. And they knew that General Putnam had borrowed them, along with Justin, only as messengers; he'd promised Jeremiah Hanson that they would not be involved in the fighting.

But as Andrew and Nathan looked around, they saw boys their own age digging fortifications down the hill to Stark's defensive position. They saw boys their own age bearing muskets along the parapet of the redoubt that they and their fathers and neighbors had built during the night.

Andrew and Nathan looked at each other for a moment as these thoughts flashed through their minds. Then, in unspoken agreement, they looked at Colonel Prescott.

Andrew spoke first. "We want to help, Colonel," he said.

"We sure do," Nathan agreed.

Colonel Prescott looked at the two for a long moment. Then his tired face broke into a grateful smile. "We sure could use you, if you're still willing to be messengers," he said. "I'll need news from Colonel Stark, and he'll need news from this part of our lines. But when the British approach, you boys get on your horses and ride out — fast! Don't make me break my promise to Jeremiah Hanson."

"Yes sir," they chorused in unison. Then they turned to Amos Burns.

"Let's go," he said.

"Wait a minute!" Nathan said, "we've got to get our rifles!"

"But get away before the British hit our lines!" Colonel Prescott insisted.

"Yes, sir," Andrew answered. He and Nathan ran to the wagon under which they'd slept for a few hours, and scooped up their rifles, powder horns, and bullet pouches. Then they trotted after Amos as the stocky farmer led them down the hill two hundred yards to the rear of the redoubt.

Already the Virginians could see the amazing speed with which the hardy New England farmers could throw up earthen fortifications. A line was being dug down the hill, from the redoubt to the rail fence that Stark's New Hampshire riflemen and some Connecticut troops had further fortified with stones. The militia had also placed two small cannon behind the fortified fence. Then, Stark had looked again at the American lines and had seen that there was still a gap between the water and the end of the fortified fence. He ordered his men at once to build a stone wall to close this gap. Here he posted his best riflemen, right beside the river.

As the three young men ran down the hill past this frenzied activity, Amos told them about the desperate problem with ammunition.

"Colonel's Stark's men only have about fifteen shots apiece," he said. "We used up all ours in target practice 'cause all our units were promised we'd get more. But we didn't. Finally, in Cambridge, we melted down the organ pipes from the church, and we made our own bullets. Then we got a gill of powder for each man."

"That's not much!" Andrew said, shocked at the thought that the American riflemen would have to face the fully equipped British soldiers without adequate ammunition.

"Well, maybe not for the Massachusetts militia it ain't," Amos said, "but we're New Hampshire riflemen. I reckon we'll make do."

The Virginians exchanged glances. Since their arrival in New York they'd been told repeatedly that the New Hampshire riflemen were very good. And they'd always known that the Pennsylvanians bragged that their riflemen were the best in the world. Virginians, of course, knew otherwise — but, wisely, Andrew and Nathan said nothing.

Now they'd reached the bottom of the hill. Here they ran to Colonel Stark and relayed Colonel Prescott's orders.

"Fine, men," the veteran officer said. "Stick with me. I think the British are going to hit us here, and I want to send you to Colonel Prescott with the news as soon as they do. We've got a good position now — we've fortified the rail fence with stones, and built a stone fence to the water's edge. As long as our ammunition holds out, the redcoats will have a tough time getting through these lines."

Meanwhile, Justin was about to bear a message to Colonel Prescott in the redoubt. Justin had been down in Charleston with the sharpshooter's who awaited the British attack, when the sergeant to whom he'd been assigned had sent him back with a message.

"Run back to Colonel Prescott, Justin!" the sergeant had said. "Tell him the British are firing at our sharpshooters. And they're deploying cannon!"

So Justin had raced up the hill to the redoubt, where he'd found the Colonel.

"The British are firing at our men in Charleston, Sir," he told the Colonel breathlessly. "And they're bringing up cannon."

Colonel Prescott nodded, then turned as another warning reached him. "The British are about to attack!" an officer shouted as he looked through his telescope at the redcoated formations below.

"All right, Justin," Colonel Prescott said. "Our cannon just arrived — and they're pitiful! Four little six-pounders! Six-pounders against the big cannons the British bring against us!"

Just then, Justin saw a dramatic figure stride rapidly and decisively into the redoubt and approach Colonel Prescott. The distinguished blond haired man was dressed in white satin breeches and pale blue waistcoat, and carried a musket.

"Who's that civilian?" Justin asked a nearby militiaman.

"That's no civilian," the man replied. "That's Dr. Joseph Warren. He's just been appointed Major General. He'll probably take command. Don't you know about him?" the man asked incredulously.

"Nope," Justin said, "I'm from New York."

"Well, I'm surprised everyone doesn't know about Dr. Warren," the man said. "He's a doctor — the most famous around. He's the one who made people take inoculations 'gainst small-pox. He stayed with some of his patients for months while they recovered. But hundreds and hundreds of people who wouldn't get inoculated died. In fact, he risked his life to nurse them through. He's one of the leaders of the patriots here, and he's a great man. And he also rode to warn the militia when the

British marched to Concord to destroy our guns. And he fought with the militia that drove the redcoats back to Boston."

"So he'll be in charge of all the units here?" Justin asked.

"I 'spect so," the man answered.

But he was wrong. As Dr. Warren stepped up to Colonel Prescott, Prescott saluted him, and offered him his command. But Dr. Warren — Maj. General Warren — declined. "I shall take no command here," he said. "I came as a volunteer with my musket to serve under you." So saying, the famous doctor and patriot leader who was already a hero to the Americans stepped up to the firing platform of the redoubt and joined the men there.

On the beach below them, General Howe had been surveying the American fortifications ever since he'd landed with the first wave of British troops. A dark frown wreathed his face: he didn't like what he saw. What he and the other British Generals said could not be done in a night — had been done! The colonists had built a real fort, they'd also constructed a formidable fence of stone and rails to cover the flank of the redoubt Howe had determined to strike. In fact, they had fortified the very point he'd planned to attack!

Snapping his telescope shut, he turned to his aide. "We need those reinforcements now. Signal for them to be rowed over at once!"

The aide ran to the signalmen who stood some distance behind the lines of infantrymen. They sprang to action at once, sending orders by signal flags for more troops to be brought to join the British assaulting force.

This delay allowed the Americans to strengthen their fortifications. But it also added to the numbers of men they would
have to face when the British finally mounted their attack.

With the prospect of more redcoats to support his attack on
the American fortifications, General Howe began to relax. He
and his officers broke open a bottle of wine, offered toasts to
their coming victory over the rebellion, and began to jest about
the coming action. The formidable lines of redcoated men, with
their white breeches and bayonet-tipped muskets, increased the
officers' sense of assurance. They knew that no militia in the
world could face the British redcoats who marched deliberately
toward their foe, firing volleys as they approached before
finally charging with the deadly bayonets.

"Those farmers will run soon enough, General," one of his
subalterns joked, "as soon as our volleys reach 'em." He raised
his glass in tribute to his chief.

"Those that don't run then will *fly* when the see the line of
steel coming at their throats!" a major said, lifting his wine-
glass to toast the certain success of their attack.

General Howe laughed. "Gentlemen, you're both right. Our
left and center forces will crush them on the first charge, and
force them out of their redoubt. Meanwhile, our attack here on
our right — on the Americans' left flank — will flush out those
riflemen behind their fence, and put us in the rear of the rebel
forces. Green troops like these militia always panic when
trained units get in their rear. We'll end the rebellion this
afternoon!"

CHAPTER TWELVE

"DON'T FIRE TILL YOU SEE THE WHITES OF THEIR EYES!"

The Americans watched grimly as the British reinforcements began to arrive on the Charleston shore, ferried hastily across the water in the Navy's small boats. The troops were the Forty Seventh Foot and the First Marines, and as soon as they got on shore, these elite units formed quickly and were sent to extend the left flank of the British lines.

And now the British were ready. As the scarlet-clad formations marched to the assault position, almost enveloping the American lines, General Howe called out to the men under his command at the extreme right of the British lines. "Behave like Englishmen! I shall not desire any one of you to go a step farther than I go myself at your head." The men cheered him as they marched up.

General Howe was one of the most famous battlefield leaders in the army of the King and his mere presence gave immense confidence to the troops. With him at their head, they could not fail!

"Tell the artillery to commence firing!" General Howe called.

Immediately the British howitzers which the boats had brought over began to add their thunder to the already continuous firing of the ships' cannons and the guns of the British batteries on floats and in Boston. Then, just as suddenly, the field guns stopped firing.

"What's the matter?" Howe blazed.

An aide ran to the guns to discern the reason for their silence. After a few hurried words with an artillery officer, the aide ran back to General Howe.

"They sent the wrong shot for the guns, General!" he cried as he approached. "They sent twelve pound shot — and our field pieces fire six pound shot!"

Howe swore.

Meanwhile, American snipers in the buildings in the town of Charleston had found the massed formations of British troops to be very good targets. Marksmen fired, reloaded, and fired again; redcoats were falling to the ground from the rigid British lines. But the lines did not falter.

The American forces that awaited the British assault totaled almost fifteen hundred men and boys. They were, for the most part, companies drawn from the militia regiments. Some of them had been very well trained for the past two years — but they were still, primarily, civilians. They had with them six small cannon.

The British force facing the militia was a professional army of twenty-five hundred soldiers and marines. About half the British troops were deployed under General Pigot on the British left, and the other half under General Howe on the British right.

General Pigot's task was to climb the hill and storm the American right and center — the redoubt. General Howe's force was to strike the center and left of the American lines, the breastworks and the rail fence that ran down the hill and ended on the Mystic River. Howe planned to burst through the American barricade, scatter the militiamen before him, then turn left and sweep up the hill toward the American redoubt from the rear — just as General Pigot's troops attacked it from the opposite side.

Howe rearranged his units, selecting the elite Light Infantry and Grenadiers to hit the left flank of the American lines where the fortified fence ran to the river. The British Light Infantry were on the British extreme right, by the water's edge. The Light Infantry, three hundred and fifty troops, marched in columns of four along the shore of the Mystic River, as the Grenadiers marched on their left.

Sweating profusely under the hot sun, the silent ranks of militiamen dressed in tan and brown awaited the onslaught of their foes.

On the British left and center, the heavily laden infantrymen moved in their rigid lines across the green fields. Fences dotted the landscape, and the ranks slowed as the men climbed these, then moved on. Citizens in Boston across the water, and the Americans on Breed's Hill above the advancing regiments, could see the precision and order of the highly drilled professional troops. Militiamen licked their lips nervously, suddenly parched with thirst, as the grim ranks marched inexorably toward them.

Standing in the redoubt beside Colonel Prescott, Justin gulped in awe at the approaching British soldiers. The redcoats' lines extended across the ground covered by the redoubt, as well as to the right of the American fortification.

Suddenly the Americans on the hill were startled by the first of the volleys fired by the marching British infantry. Some men fired back instinctively, only to be shouted at by their officers. "Wait!" the officers yelled, over and over again. "Don't fire till we command!"

The British loaded as they marched, and fired another volley at the Americans on the hill above. American officers leaped to the parapet and ran along it, kicking up those muskets some of their militiamen were aiming. "Don't fire!" they yelled again. "Wait til they're in range!"

Now the green fields were covered not only by the bright red-jacketed troops, but also by clouds of smoke from the volleys of the approaching British.

The heat was intense. So was the fear.

On the hill above, the Americans marveled at the redcoats who could march with such heavy packs on their backs, fire in massed volleys, climb the fences that obstructed their path, and continue their implacable approach toward the American redoubt.

Ships' cannons thundered continuously, adding to the terror — but their balls were still unable to reach the American lines. Only those that rebounded along the ground and climbed the hill as they bounced posed any danger to the waiting Americans. Floating British batteries in the water, and those on the Copp's Hill on the Boston shore, added their fire to that of the mighty ships' broadsides. The Americans licked their dry lips as the grim lines of professional soldiers came closer and closer.

When will we fire? Justin asked himself anxiously.

"Fire!" Colonel Prescott shouted. The American lines flamed with the deadly volley. Rank upon rank of the approaching redcoats crumpled to the ground. The British formations staggered, then halted in great confusion. Officers and noncoms shouted for the men behind to fill the ranks of those who'd been struck down. Hastily they formed their lines again, and, on command, fired another volley at the militiamen behind the redoubt. But, like their other volleys, this one too went high, and few of the American were struck.

Then the ranks of British troops were ready to resume their march. Maddened by the effects of the American fire, stung by the spectacle of civilian farmers firing at the army of the King, the enraged soldiers and marines fired their muskets in regular volleys as they marched in quick step to assault the American positions.

When the redcoated ranks were close, the Americans fired again, their muskets loaded with shot, nails, whatever missiles they could cram into the barrels. Again the British lines seemed to crumple. The devastated formations shuddered, halted — then began to retreat! The retreat became a panic as the British soldiers simply fled down the hill, heedless of formation, impervious to their officers shouted orders to halt and reform.

Seeing the collapse of their enemies' lines, the Americans in the redoubt cheered as they fired, reloaded, and fired again. Below them, the shattered English formations fled rapidly down the hill, leaving the ground covered with their wounded and dead comrades.

The uninjured British officers were unable to halt the frenzied retreat of the fleeing redcoats. With tears of rage and shame at their frantic flight, officers flayed the panic-stricken men with the flat sides of their swords, screaming for them to halt and reform. But the stumbling mobs of disorganized soldiers paid them no heed — the rout continued.

General Pigot's attack on the American redoubt had been beaten off.

But on the extreme right of the British lines, and simultaneously with General Pigot's attack on the redoubt, the gallant General Howe led his elite Grenadiers and Light Infantry along the beach toward the American rail fence.

"We'll drive them before us," he called again to his men, "then turn left and climb the hill and assault the redoubt from the rear! Those rebels will be shattered and their rebellion will be over!" Howe himself led the formations in the center directly against the American breastwork.

Behind the fortified breastwork and rail fences, the American marksmen waited silently to receive General Howe's attack. The river was to their left, the fortified hill to their right, and before them was the chilling spectacle of the relentlessly approaching dreaded Light Infantry and the Grenadiers with their tall bearskin hats. Again and again the American officers reminded their men not to fire until ordered to do so. Old Isaac Putnam prowled the American lines, yelling to his men, "Don't fire until you see the whites of their eyes! Then, fire low!"

Suddenly, before the British troops reached firing range, Colonel Stark ran out forty yards from the stone-fortified fence. Here he stopped and drove a stake into the ground. Turning to face his men, his back to the approaching Grenadiers and Light Infantry, he called to his marksmen to look at the stake.

"Not a man is to fire until the first British regular passes this stake!" he yelled. Then the gallant Colonel ran back to join his men as the British lines drew rapidly closer. His men cheered him as he leaped the fence and rejoined them.

Andrew and Nathan stood with Amos some distance behind the lines of American militiamen who manned the rail fence. Andrew suddenly realized that his mouth was dry — and not just because of the heat. He was scared. Nathan was too. They gripped their rifles in sweaty hands and waited.

Suddenly Amos spoke. "Man, this is scary!" He glanced at the two Virginians. They agreed. Then the three turned their eyes back to look over the lines of crouching militiamen: the British columns were almost within range.

The two small American cannon fired at the approaching Light Infantry. Men fell, but the formations came on rapidly. These Light Infantrymen and Grenadiers were men who'd been humiliated in the disastrous retreat from Lexington just two months before, and they were burning to avenge themselves on those rebel farmers who'd driven them back to Boston in shameful defeat.

One hundred yards from the rail fence, General Howe halted the advance, and ordered the troops to move out of column and form lines for the assault. Sweat-sodden soldiers moved with practiced precision into their attack formations as the noncoms dressed the lines.

This movement prompted some of the Americans to fire. Their officers yelled at once for them to cease. "Wait!" they shouted.

"Wait til you see the whites of their eyes!" Old Isaac Putnam called again. "I'll shoot the first man who pulls trigger before he's ordered! We'll fire together — and mow 'em down!"

Clouds of smoke burst from the approaching British soldiers as the lines of British troops began to fire in volley while they marched. With implacable precision the redcoated Light Infantry — and the greencoated Grenadiers — rapidly closed with the waiting militiamen. But the American officers had their men in control now, and the silent lines of farmers and shopkeepers, fathers and sons, schoolteachers and craftsmen waited behind their fortified fence as the world's finest professional troops rushed toward them. The volleys of the marching British were nerve-wracking. But they were not yet accurate, passing over the heads of the waiting Americans.

Andrew felt the heat from the sun beat down on his head. A slight breeze from the river to his left failed to bring relief. The bright sun flamed down on the drama as the British ships shattered the air with their regular broadsides. Clouds of smoke rolled across the waters toward the land. Frightened gulls added their screams to the dreadful noise.

Andrew and Nathan had loaded their rifles when Amos had loaded his. The three boys stood by a wagon of supplies behind the American lines and watched the British troops come closer and closer in their terrifying quick-step, naked bayonets out thrust before them.

"When will we fire back?" Andrew asked, his face anguished at the sight of the implacably approaching British.

"Why don't we shoot 'em as they come?" Nathan asked.

"Because our officers want our volleys to have the most effect when we fire," Amos answered. "It's scary to wait like this, but it means that the men have a chance to take good aim. And when they fire all at once, it knocks down the front ranks, and that makes the British stop and reform their lines.

The British were just fifty yards away. And now they were running rapidly toward the fence, the deadly line of bayonets thrust forward. The Welsh Fusiliers in the lead, the Light Infantry behind, the Grenadiers with their tall hats were on the British left.

Then the running soldiers reached the stake Colonel Stark had driven into the ground.

"Fire!" bellowed General Putnam.

The thunderous volley flamed from the massed rifles behind the fence. A cloud of smoke from the expended black powder billowed across the sand toward the advancing infantrymen. The British formations staggered as the cloud of shot swept through them like a scythe, and whole rows of men crumpled to the ground. In the ensuing confusion, the surviving officers and noncoms rushed about to reform the English lines, shoving men from The King's Own Regiment into the place of the fallen. Then they ordered their men to return the American fire. A ragged volley flashed from the new-formed ranks.

The British practice was to fire by volley as they advanced, getting closer to the enemy with each volley. Then, as the enemy reloaded, the British would charge and break their opponents formations with the bayonet. But the Americans were firing with such rapidity that the British found no space between volleys for reforming their shattered lines and launching a charge.

For as the Americans who'd fired the first volley stepped back from the breastworks and fences to reload, another line of men took their place. While the first rank reloaded their rifles, the second rank took aim at the approaching redcoats.

"Fire!"

Another volley flashed from the Americans. Whole lines of British soldiers once more fell to the ground. The others hesitated.

The British officers realized that they could no longer allow the Americans to fire another such murderous volley. They had to charge with the bayonet.

"Now, men!" they cried, as again they reformed the shattered lines. "Give 'em the bayonet before they reload. Charge!"

But another line of militiamen with loaded guns had taken the place of those who had just fired, and a third deadly volley boomed from the American lines.

And now the British formations faced a kind of fire they'd never encountered before. The Americans were no longer firing by volley, with significant periods of silence between as they reloaded their guns — periods the English usually used for their bayonet charge. Now, as fast as each militiaman could aim, shoot, and reload, he did so. The men were packed together along the fence, their long muskets and rifles blazing away at the crumbling British lines. Soon a continuous deadly fire was flaming from the rail fence.

The shattered British ranks could take it no more. The decimated formations halted in confusion. Then, terrified, the Light Infantrymen and Grenadiers began to retreat along the beach.

Where Howe led, the Grenadiers still fought their way forward against the American fire. Then Howe's officers began to go down under the dreadful fire. Again and again Howe shouted for his men to form and charge. Soon every one of his officers was on the ground, wounded or dying. Packs of men staggered in confusion under the relentless American musketry, struggling with the walking wounded, helping shattered men to the rear. Smoke covered the ground, making men cough, the noise of the guns deafened and stunned them all, and the ground was strewn with ranks of bloodied red and white and green uniformed wounded and dead British soldiers.

The survivors of the Light Infantry formations broke ranks and fled from the devastating American fire.

Howe ordered his remaining Grenadiers to retreat.

Shouting triumphantly, the Americans continued to load and fire as fast as they could. Suddenly a group of militiamen began to climb the fence to pursue the fleeing British.

"Stop! Stop!" their officers yelled, as with difficulty they forced the excited men to return to their barricade. They could not afford to let their men break ranks, then be caught in a possible British counter-attack in the open field. Determinedly, the militia officers kept their restless shouting men behind the fence.

Andrew, Nathan, and Amos found themselves cheering with all their strength as the surviving British troops stumbled out of range. Then the boys themselves began to cough as the wind from the river blew into their faces the clouds of smoke that covered the militia lines.

The militiamen were yelling in triumph as the fleeing British soldiers ran out of range, but their officers called for order.

"It's not over!" Colonel Stark insisted. "They're not through with us yet! But they've learned a lesson, boys, that's for sure! They've learned a lesson!" The men were grinning, and the stern face of the Colonel began to grin back.

"Load up, men!" General Putnam called, striding along the American lines. "Let's be ready for 'em when they come again!"

In the redoubt atop Breed's Hill, the shouting Americans cheered wildly as General Pigot's regiments on the British left flank fled down the slopes, leaving the field strewn with their dead and wounded. Muskets were thrown every which way by the retreating English soldiers. The once splendid regiments were demoralized mobs of panic-stricken men now. Their surviving officers and noncoms shouted desperately for the men to form again in proper order, but to no avail. Nothing could stop the survivors as they stumbled in retreat, with the taunting cheers of the victorious Americans ringing in their ears.

The colonials in the redoubt were jubilant, cheering again and again. They'd met the fabled British army — and sent it reeling in disorder down the hill! Colonel Prescott moved among them, praising them for their courage in standing fast and mowing down the British troops. Men coughed and wiped the tears from their eyes as the clouds of smoke from their muskets hung over their lines.

"But it's not over!" Prescott called again and again. "Load up. Form up. Stay ready!"

He glanced around at the men inside the redoubt, and his jaw tightened. There were only about one hundred and fifty men left. Many had drifted off, some to help the wounded get away, others to look for ammunition. Others had just vanished.

Prescott's men on the hill, and Putnam's and Stark's men on the slope and along the beach, reloaded their guns and made ready to fight again.

The British had suffered a stunning defeat — in plain sight of thousands of spectators watching from the roof tops of Boston and the surrounding land! The Americans knew that pride alone would force the English generals to attack again.

And the American militiamen were tired. They'd marched for hours the day before, they'd dug through the night and then through the morning hours, they'd fought the renowned red-coats to a standstill and defeated them.

Small groups of men left the American redoubt on the hill, and the fences that led down' behind it to the river, as able-bodied men helped the walking wounded retreat to Bunker Hill. Andrew saw groups carrying in blankets those who were unable to walk. But the number of wounded and killed militia-man at this stage of the battle was small indeed compared to the hundreds of British casualties who lay on the fields before them.

Now, the militiamen were tired. And thirsty. They couldn't seem to get enough water.

Nor powder. They were almost out of gunpowder and bullets.

☆ **CHAPTER THIRTEEN** ☆

AGAIN THE REDCOATS CHARGE!

"Andrew, run this message to Colonel Prescott right away!" General Putnam said, as he handed the Virginian a folded paper.

"Yes, sir," Andrew said. He turned and began to trot up the hill, past the line of breast-works behind which the American militia awaited a second British attack.

Behind him, the General turned to Nathan. "Nathan, come with me. We've got to move men from Bunker Hill to reinforce Colonel Prescott in the redoubt."

And now began one of the bitterest experiences of General Putnam's and Nathan's lives. For when they reached the fortified lines on Bunker's Hill, they learned that not all of the American militiamen were willing to help their comrades on Breed's Hill face the next British attack.

General Putnam stormed among the ranks, trying to shame units into marching with him to join Colonel Prescott. "Your comrades have mowed the redcoats down!" he shouted, waving his sword. "They need help. They need more gunpowder and bullets. And they need you! Follow me, men, and we'll send the British packing once more!"

But few agreed to follow the general back to Breed's Hill. In utter frustration he called one officer a plain coward, then led the few volunteers forward, finally rejoining Colonel Prescott in the redoubt. Andrew had brought General Putnam's message, and had then remained in the redoubt for further orders, leaning against the dirt wall and observing the British troops below. Nathan joined Andrew as the two officers conferred.

"Any ammunition, General?" Prescott asked hopefully.

"None, Colonel," Putnam replied in bitter sadness. "None. And only these few men were willing to come with me. You'll have to face the British with what you've got."

"We've got few bullets and little powder left," said Prescott, his eyes squinting in the sun. "Our men did the enemy great damage — but they used up most all their ammunition in doing it. We won't be able to hold this redoubt if the British push their attack."

Andrew was shocked as he overheard these words. "Why won't the militia on Bunker Hill come, Nathan," he asked quietly.

"I don't know," Nathan replied, his hazel eyes clouded with the memory of those men who'd refused to follow General Putnam to Breed's Hill. He took off his hat and wiped the sweat from his face. "Most of 'em wouldn't budge. One fat militia colonel was lying on the ground — said he was exhausted from the march. General Putnam called him a coward! Right to his face! And the fat colonel just took it! You never saw a man so mad as General Putnam then! He knocked some of the militia down with the flat of his sword and called them cowards too.

But it didn't do any good. Most of 'em wouldn't come. A few came, though. He brought them back with him."

"Then why wouldn't they send bullets and powder to the men who're here?" Andrew asked. "These men are willing to fight. They just need powder and bullets."

"They said they didn't have enough for themselves."

"But if they're not going to fight, they won't **need** bullets and powder for themselves!" Andrew said in exasperation.

"That's what the General told 'em," Nathan said. "But their officers wouldn't listen. They won't come, and they won't send ammunition."

The two Virginians stood in silence as they pondered this. Around them, wounded men were being carried back to Bunker Hill.

"Come back when you get those men to the wagons!" Colonel called after them.

"Why's he saying that?" Andrew asked.

"Cause some of the men from here who help take the wounded back to Bunker Hill don't come back," Nathan replied. "Some of them just stay there."

Down below the hills, on the level ground leading from the water, the British generals moved rapidly to prepare their troops for another assault. Officers from Boston had been pressed into service to replace those who had fallen. Roaming the lines of his dazed troops, General Howe shouted out orders, reforming the shattered regiments on the British right, while

General Pigot and his remaining officers regrouped the regiments on the left.

Howe determined to shift the aim of his attack from the fence along the beach where so many of his elite troops had fallen. "That position's too strong!" he told his surviving officers. "We'll aim more to the left. We'll storm those breastworks that extended up the hill!"

Then he asked himself again: *How'd those Americans build such fortifications overnight? Our army couldn't do it — no army could. And where'd they learn to fire so fast? Our soldiers can't do that!*

Shaking his head in disbelief, the grim veteran swiftly sketched out his plans for his new officers. "We'll storm that breastwork leading up the hill," he called out, "scatter the rebels there, then swing left and hit the redoubt from the rear!"

Rapidly Howe put the British formations in order. And on the British left and center, General Pigot again ordered his regiments in motion toward the American redoubt. This time, he extended his lines even more, so that they threatened to encircle the redoubt and cut off all retreat from Breed's to Bunker Hill. The lines of redcoated, white trousered men, still bearing their heavy packs with three full days of rations, moved obediently forward, bitterly shamed at their first retreat, determined to crush the Americans with their bayonets.

But the American snipers in the buildings of Charleston, right on the shore opposite Boston, were shooting down too many of the English soldiers. Exasperated, General Pigot sent a messenger by boat to Admiral Graves, telling him to use his cannons to destroy the town. Other messengers were sent to the

British batteries on Copp's Hill in Boston. Within half an hour, the British artillery on ship and on shore were loaded with special cartridges — cannonballs filled with hot pitch. These, hitting wooden buildings, would splatter their combustible material all over, rapidly spreading flame and destruction.

Then the guns on Copp's Hill, and the guns on the nearby warships, began firing these incendiary balls into the two hundred homes and buildings of the town of Charleston.

On the Charleston shore, the British ranks were formed again. Orders were shouted, and the entire line moved forward to the attack as the cannons on ship and in Boston continued to pound the American positions. The noise was awful as the scarlet formations began to approach the scenes of the previous slaughter.

"Take this message to General Putnam and Colonel Stark!" Prescott said suddenly to Andrew and Nathan. "Tell 'em Howe's massed his formations against their breastwork, leading up the hill. They'd better send reinforcements there!"

"Yes, sir," the Virginians said. Gripping their rifles, they ran down the hill, past the American fortifications, seeking out the officers. They found Putnam first, and passed on this news.

"Thanks, boys," the old General said, sweating heavily in the heat. "We've seen that already, and moved some men from the beach."

"Here they come!" a man yelled, and the General and the two boys looked instantly at the approaching British.

Back atop the hill, standing on the parapet of the redoubt, Colonel Prescott called Justin to his side. "Look at those regiments, boy," he said, sweeping his arm in a broad gesture from right to left. "We shattered 'em on their first charge. But that won't stop 'em. They'll come again. And probably again. Run to the right and tell the Colonel there to watch his flank. It looks like they're going to envelop us."

Gripping his rifled carbine, Justin ran swiftly toward the extreme right of the American line as the ominous scarlet-coated formations at the bottom of the hill began their second attack. The grim ranks moved implacably forward as the vengeful soldiers stepped over the bodies of their killed and wounded comrades, slipping and skidding in the pools of blood.

The thunder of British cannon increased. Then the Americans began to yell with anguish and anger as they saw the buildings of Charleston suddenly explode into flames from the British cannonade.

Watching the entire battle from a high building in Boston, the British General Burgoyne saw the awesome scene, and described this later in a letter to friends in England.

And now ensued one of the greatest scenes of war that can be conceived; if we look to the height, Howe's corps ascending the hill in the face of entrenchments and in the face of a very disadvantageous ground, was much engaged; to the left the enemy was pouring in fresh troops by thousands, over the land, and in the arm of the sea, our floating batteries cannonading them; straight before us a large and noble town in one great blaze; the church steeples being of timber, were great pyramids of fire above the rest; behind us the church steeples and height of our own camp, covered with spectators of the rest of our army who

*were (not) engaged; the hills round the country covered
with spectators, the enemy all in anxious suspense; the
roar of cannon, mortars, and musketry, the crush of
churches, ships upon the stocks, and whole streets falling
together in ruin to fill the ear; the storm of the redoubts
with the objects above described to fill the eye, and the re-
flection that perhaps a defeat was the final loss to the British Empire in America, to fill the mind, made the whole a
picture and complication of horror and importance beyond anything that ever came to my lot to be witness to. . . .*

General Burgoyne's fancy ran away with him here: there
were no "thousands" of American reinforcements pouring into
the American lines. Two companies only came from the hundreds of militiamen still on Bunker Hill, and these brought
ammunition only for themselves, not for the almost powder-
less men on Breed's Hill.

Now, on the entire front, the British regiments advanced
through the tall grass, the men stumbling over the bodies of
their fallen comrades, their boots slipping in the blood-covered
ground. But on they came, a grim, curving line of ordered
steel-tipped regiments, heading again with resolute purpose
toward the militia crouched in the redoubt and behind the
breastworks and fences along the hill beyond.

Justin reached the officer on the American right and passed
on Prescott's order. Then he ran back to the center of the
redoubt, his feet kicking up dust as he ran, dodging sweating
men as these saw to their muskets and prepared to receive the
next British attack. Justin thought his ears would be deafened
by the thunder of the British cannonade. Just as he reached the
redoubt he heard Colonel Prescott shout, "Fire!"

The redoubt flamed again with a massed volley. Smoke and iron swept down the hill toward the redcoats just thirty yards away. The breastwork down the hill flamed and thundered also. In the entire encircling British line, whole ranks of redcoated soldiers were swept again to the ground under the disciplined short-range American fire. The English formations staggered as huge gaps appeared in their lines, and wounded men cried out as they fell.

Then the American militiamen gave place to others with loaded guns, and another wall of flame and shot struck the attacking regiments.

And now the Americans facing the forces under General Pigot began to do what their comrades under Colonel Stark had done, something to which the British were not accustomed: they began to fire in a continuous fashion, men loading and shooting as fast as they could, not waiting for massed volleys, giving the advancing British no time to reform their lines and charge with the bayonet.

The redoutable British Marines faltered under the murderous fire. Then, once again, their line broke; once again redcoated men fled down the hill in demoralized clusters. Officers and noncoms shouted and screamed for them to stand, but to no avail. The devastated units fled yelling down the hill, racing desperately to escape the awful American fire. Englishmen watching from roof tops in Boston and from the ships in the harbor could not believe their eyes as they saw the world-famous marines break and flee before the American fire.

In another part of the decimated British lines, the stunned survivors of the 52nd regiment could stand the continuous American fire no more. To the utter shock of the watching

British in Boston and on the ships, they, too, broke formation, turned, and ran stumbling back down the hill. More men in the regiments to their left and right began to do the same.

Soon the entire British line was falling back, the surviving outraged officers unable to restrain their terror-stricken fleeing soldiers as they stumbled and fell over the bloody bodies of fallen comrades.

Likewise, on the British right, the forces under General Howe shuddered to a stop. Whole ranks of soldiers were mown down by the deadly American muskets and rifles. Every single one of Howe's new officers was down, most of the noncoms who took over were similarly hit, and when corporals and privates took their places, they too were struck by the American fire.

An officer who survived the defeat on the British right wrote later:

> *"Our light-infantry were served up in complete formations against the grass fence, without being able to penetrate... Most of our grenadiers and light-infantry... lost three fourths, and many nine tenths of their men. Some had only eight or nine men in a company left; some three, four, and five."*

The gallant General Howe called finally for a charge with the bayonet, pleading with his men to sweep over the American breastworks. But the continuous fire from the American rifles and muskets swept the next lines of attackers away, breaking their formations before their few remaining noncoms could form them. This continual individual firing by the Americans was devastating as well as demoralizing to them.

On the British left, General Pigot had already called for his shattered units to retreat.

General Howe at last did the same. This brave officer had borne a charmed life. But he wrote later that a darkness came suddenly over his eyes at the stark defeat of his disciplined men by the American militia. Great officer that he was, and later proved himself again to be, he said that he was never the same after this retreat.

To the dismay of the reserve regiments, and the spectators in Boston, the shattered remnants of the British formations stumbled down the hill in utter defeat.

But the American officers were now appalled by the realization that their men had hardly any ammunition left. Should the British attack a third time, there was simply not enough powder and shot to hold them off. The men would be able to fire once or twice, some three times — that was all.

CHAPTER FOURTEEN

RETREAT TO THE MAINLAND

Across the water from the battle, standing with the British batteries on Copp's Hill, the English Commander-in-Chief General Clinton watched in horror and shame as the second British attack faltered, then broke before the American fire. He shouted orders that mobilized the 2nd Marines and the Sixty-third Regiment of regular army troops, and sent them in boats to reinforce the shattered regiments on the peninsula. Then he raced to the wharf and threw himself into a boat with his aides. Quickly the boat rowed the officers across the water to the peninsula where demoralized remnants of the decimated British regiments wandered in dazed shock along the shore.

American snipers shot two of Clinton's men as they leaped from the boat and splashed ashore. But the intrepid General rallied the shaken troops, rounded up the injured who were still able to fight, and with the officers he'd brought from Boston, formed the demoralized men in line for another assault on the hill. To this point, General Clinton had been a spectator of the battle, watching from the British battery in Boston. Now he gave his defeated army an example of brilliant battle-field leadership as he reorganized them for yet another attack.

Before he arrived, the British officers had been unable to control the shattered survivors. Now, under Clinton's decisive command, the formations were brought again into order. On the right, General Howe collected the scattered units and readied them for another charge. These troops were humiliated at their bloody defeats, and burning to avenge their shame and their dreadful losses. Howe's scarlet coat and white breeches were splattered with the blood of other men, but he himself had not been scratched — yet in each assault he had marched at the front of his soldiers' lines, in the teeth of the American fire.

Coolly Howe planned this third assault from the British right. He ordered — finally — that the men drop their heavy packs on the ground. New regiments were swung into line. The Light Infantry were to fake — but not press — an attack on the deadly rail fence on the beach. To their left, the Forty-third Regiment, the Fifty-second Regiment, and the Grenadiers were ordered to storm the breastwork before which so many of their comrades had already fallen. The Thirty-eighth and Fifth Regiments were thrown into line on their left, with orders to take the American redoubt.

The British field artillery had been largely ineffective because of the swampy ground which had hindered the guns from being brought to bear. Howe now ordered the guns forward anyway, demanding they be put into position to shell the American positions with the deadly grapeshot, loads of musket balls that spread out as they were fired. These loads of iron balls could decimate any infantry formations they struck. So the British artillerists wrestled several of the heavy cannons closer to the American lines.

With four hundred fresh men in the line, and the ranks of the bloodied regiments formed again, the British were ready for their third assault on the American citizen-militia. Unlike their opponents, many of whom had no more than two shots apiece left, the British had full cartridge pouches. And all of the redcoats had bayonets.

In the American position, two companies of militia reinforcements had finally arrived from Bunker Hill to augment the shrunken force within the American redoubt. But many militiamen had left, more in fact than now remained to face the third British attack. And the companies of reinforcements had brought no ammunition for anyone but themselves. The Americans would be able to fire one volley, perhaps two — that was all.

The British regiments began to advance. Their field guns, brought forward at last, thundered furiously, sending hundreds of musket balls sailing through the air toward the waiting Americans. The ships in the harbor fired in continuous volleys, the big guns on Copp's Hill boomed relentlessly, and under this dreadful barrage the deadly rows of bayonets approached the American lines.

Colonel Stark had been watching the British advance. Suddenly he turned to Andrew, Nathan, and Justin. "You boys get your horses and take back wounded men — at once! We'll need these men to fight again! I had no right to keep you here so long! Get back and report to Jeremiah Hanson!" He glared sternly, shocked that he'd forgotten that these boys were not meant to be drawn into the fight.

"Thanks for your help," he said then, and smiled. "Get some of those wounded men back to Cambridge, though, and hurry!"

"Yes, sir," they said. The three turned and began to run up the hill to the wagon behind the redoubt where their horses were tethered. To their left they could see the approaching British regiments, the long lines closing fast. The redcoats were almost within firing range of the Americans when half-a-dozen green uniformed marksmen left the approaching British formation and ran toward the militiamen. Still out of musket range, the British sharpshooters stopped, knelt in the grass, took quick aim, and fired. The three boys saw with horror that two of the militiamen behind the fence to their left cried out and fell to the ground, their muskets falling from their hands. The British marksmen were reloading rapidly — clearly, they planned to fire again.

"Their rifles are beyond range of our mens' muskets!" Nathan cried.

"But not beyond the range of our rifles!" Andrew said grimly. "We can reach 'em!"

At once the three boys turned, took steady aim, and fired. Two of the British fell back to the ground, their rifles falling from their hands. The others, shocked, looked up from their reloading, trying to locate the marksmen who'd shot their comrades. They saw the boys at once.

"Let's go!" Andrew shouted quickly. "They'll waste their shots on us as we run!"

The three broke into a run, Andrew and Nathan reloading as they ran in the manner of the Virginia woodsmen. The four remaining British marksmen fired at the running figures, but at that distance had no chance of hitting such fast moving targets.

"Keep going, Justin!" Andrew yelled, "get the horses!"

Andrew and Nathan ground to a halt, took long breaths to steady themselves, lifted their deadly rifles, centered these again on the reloading British snipers, and fired.

Two more British marksmen fell to the ground. Then the bayonet-tipped ranks of British soldiers behind them broke into a rapid trot and passed the remaining two marksmen. With wild curses and shouts the enraged British troops charged the militia lines.

The American breastworks burst into flame at the approaching regiments, as Andrew and Nathan sprinted up the hill, reloading again as they ran. Justin had already untethered their mounts, but was having great difficulty holding them as the musket and cannon fire increased in volume.

"Grab these reins!" he yelled, and Andrew and Nathan did so, swinging into their saddles with practiced ease.

"This way!" Justin shouted, pointing to a group of wounded men limping wearily toward Bunker Hill. "Let's pick up three of them!"

The boys trotted their horses after the walking men, and pulled up beside them. "We can ride three of you," Justin said.

The men looked up gratefully. Then each boy reached down a hand and helped a wounded man to mount behind him. Two red-hot cannonballs bounced suddenly in front of them, and the horses skipped aside, almost throwing their riders.

"Let's go!" Justin said to the man behind him. "Hold on!" He kicked his horse into a run.

As the three horses with their double loads ran toward the neck of the peninsula that led to the mainland, the riders heard behind them, from all along the American lines, the thunder of continuous musket-fire. Their horses shied again, but the riders gripped the reins firmly and kept them on course. The man behind Nathan almost fell off, but Nathan reached an arm around and helped him keep his seat. "Grab me around the waist," Nathan said.

Behind them, the American militiamen had once more waited until the British were in point-blank range. Again the slaughter in the red coated ranks was terrible. Those Americans with ammunition reloaded rapidly. And from the breastworks behind the redoubt, and the rail and stone fences that led to the water, they fired once more with deadly effect. Again the redcoats' lines staggered and halted. Again and again their remaining officers and noncoms directed their ragged volleys against the murderous but now faltering American fire. Smoke roared out from the lines of guns, often obscuring the targets against which they were aimed.

But, for the men in the redoubt, the next volley for many of the militiamen was the last — most of these men had exhausted their ammunition. Suddenly the American fire from the redoubt went out as suddenly as it had begun, like a candle snuffed out in the night.

The shouting redcoats charged the American fort from three directions. At the head of the British marines the gallant Major John Pitcairn, wounded twice in the preceding attacks, went down for the last time, his body struck by four bullets. His son rushed to the fallen leader and cradled the fallen major's head in his arms.

"I have lost my father!" he cried.

"We have lost *our* father!" the marines replied, as they clambered over the walls and leaped for the Americans within, determined to avenge their admired fallen major.

"Give them steel!" the British officers cried, waving their swords as the redcoats climbed the walls of the redoubt.

Swarms of enraged soldiers climbed up the parapet, even as others fought their way over the breastwork. Many Americans, well-trained Massachusetts militia, used their own bayonets to fight off the hordes of British. But many others had no bayonets.

"Club 'em with your guns!" Colonel Prescott roared, showing his skill by almost decapitating a British soldier with a vicious swing of his sword. "Grab their muskets from 'em" he shouted as he slashed another redcoat with his blood-stained blade. Inspired, the militiamen fought then like tigers, swinging their muskets against the bayonet-armed British, felling many of them. Other Americans threw their empty muskets in the faces of the English, then wrestled the bayonet-tipped muskets from the enemy and used them themselves.

General Pigot, commanding the English left, was too small to climb into the American positions with his men. He ran to a nearby tree, climbed into the branches, and swung into the redoubt, urging his men to mow down the militiamen. From three sides, now, hundreds of British soldiers poured over the walls of the redoubt and the breastworks that had served the Americans so well.

Colonel Prescott fought coolly, parrying bayonet thrusts with great skill as he wielded his sword with deadly effect. Again and again he struck aside the the enemies' naked steel, and cut down the English soldiers.

"Get out!" he called finally to his men. "Fall back!" With calm courage he led a formation of militiamen through the press of confused combatants toward the exit.

More redcoats poured into the redoubt, and soon the dust from hundreds of tramping feet rose in the air, choking, stifling, blinding, so that many Americans could not see the open port through which to escape. But scores of militiamen stood fast and fought with their clubbed muskets, allowing many of their comrades to escape.

Colonel Prescott passed the striking figure of General Warren who was also directing a group fighting to cover the American withdrawal. Then Prescott and his men were outside, moving down the hill in good order, fighting off the British with sword and clubbed muskets. Below the redoubt on the hill, from the now-captured breastwork, the Americans retreated, fighting fiercely behind fences and obstructions, contesting the British advance in a bitter withdrawal. The men behind the rail fence remained fighting at their positions, however, waiting until they saw that the Americans on the hill had made their way clear. Then they too began to conduct a careful, skillful, fighting retreat, slowing the charging British units, buying time for the militiamen from the hill to escape.

And now Nathan, Andrew, and Justin rode with their wounded passengers across the narrow neck of land that connected the peninsula to the mainland. Again they felt the full force of the deadly cannonade from the British warships.

Retreating men in their brown homespun clothes were struck down repeatedly by the savage naval barrage aimed at them from His Majesty's vessels in the Mystic River to the north, and from the ships in the Bay to the south. Red hot cannon balls flashed from the ships, bounded along the ground, knocking down any militiamen in their way and gouging great furrows wherever they struck. The noise was indescribable. Smoke drifted over the peninsula from the continuous barrages of the naval cannon, and the acrid fumes made the fleeing men cough.

Oh, Lord, Andrew prayed fervently, *please let us cross this peninsula!* Nathan and Justin were praying the same thing.

Finally the riders reached the mainland. And now at last they were free from the dreadful shot from the British guns. Andrew looked back quickly and saw on the Charleston side groups of militiamen still fighting off the pursuing British regiments. And now he saw large numbers of brown clothed militiamen lying on the ground, from the neck of the peninsula back to the hills beyond.

The Americans suffered their greatest losses during the retreat, as they withdrew from the pursuing British under the deadly fire of grapeshot from the ships' guns as well as from the massed volleys of the advancing regiments.

"We just made it!" Nathan said gratefully to the man hanging grimly onto him.

"Thank the Lord for that!" his passenger said.

The majority of the American militiamen had fought their way free because of the bravery and tenacity of the men behind the rail fence as well as the other disciplined units that continued to turn and hold off the pursuing British. Colonel Gardner had led his men in a skillful covering fight so that the troops on Breed's Hill might escape. When he was shot down, his second in command, Major Jackson, took command. Jackson gathered other scattered units and led them in a fine fighting retreat, delaying the British advance so that hundreds of militiamen could escape to the mainland.

On Bunker Hill, General Putnam had tried to rally the men to fight off the advancing British, but it had been no use. The charging regiments drove the militiamen from that height, shooting down many of the men in homespun as they retreated.

Still the British advance was slowed by tenacious tactical leadership of small units of colonial militiamen. Finally, the bulk of the Americans crossed the shot-swept Charleston Neck and reached the safety of the mainland.

"Look!" Justin shouted suddenly, pulling his horse to a halt and pointing back to the peninsula. "The British have stopped!"

Andrew and Nathan stopped their horses also, and turned. It was true. The British formations had halted. The officers could no longer drive the exhausted men forward. Whole ranks stumbled to the ground, gasping for breath, utterly spent. The British had taken thirty Americans prisoner. Later it was learned that two hundred and seventy American militiamen had been wounded, and a hundred had been killed.

But the British army had suffered in terrible proportion to the numbers they'd committed to the action. Out of a total of two thousand five hundred soldiers and marines thrown into battle, a thousand and fifty men and been killed and wounded.

From the point of view of casualties as a percentage of men engaged — forty-two percent — it was the bloodiest tactical loss the British were ever to suffer in that war.

But Breed's Hill and Bunker Hill, and the whole of the Charleston Peninsula, had fallen to the British. The town of Charleston had been burned to the ground, its two hundred houses and buildings destroyed.

The battleground belonged to the armies of England's King.

The three exhausted boys delivered their wounded to a field hospital on the edge of Cambridge. Then, they trotted their horses into town and rode to the headquarters building to report to Jeremiah Hanson.

Hanson's tired face broke into a wide smile as he saw them ride up. "Am I glad to see you men!" he exclaimed.

"We're glad to be back, Mr. Hanson," Justin said for the three of them as they dismounted stiffly.

"You got caught in that battle!" It was a statement, not a question.

"Yes, sir," Justin replied. "We did. We'd been carrying messages for the officers when the British first attacked. Then, when they attacked for the third time, Colonel Stark sent us back with some wounded men."

"Well, I thank the Lord that you're safe," Hanson said. "I couldn't have faced your father — or my conscience — otherwise."

Then Hanson was all business. "You've got to hurry. I want you to ride out of town at once — head back without delay! Militia units are streaming back now, and no one here knows what the British are going to do. We've learned that they suffered terrible casualties — many more than we did. But they're disciplined troops, and, unlike our men, they have plenty of ammunition. Our units are demoralized, and if the English come after us now it could be bad. You boys have got to get going."

"What about the wagons, Mr. Hanson?" Andrew asked.

"They've already gone," Hanson replied. "You don't have to worry about them. Just get yourselves back to Newport." Then he looked at them sharply. "Have you eaten anything?" he asked.

"No, sir," Nathan replied. The others said the same. They hadn't eaten anything since early morning — they hadn't had time to think about eating, in fact. Now, they realized that they were practically starving!

"Wait here," Hanson said abruptly. He turned and hurried back into the headquarters building. In a few moments he emerged from the door, carrying a basket. "Here's meat, bread, cheese, and apple cider. More than even you three boys can down at one sitting! Take this with you — don't eat it now, 'cause you've got to get away from here! But when you get out of town, dig in!"

He handed Justin the basket. Then he shook hands with the three, and waved them off with heartfelt thanks for all that they'd done for the Patriot cause.

And now darkness was falling. As the three boys had ridden from town, they'd feasted on the food Hanson had given them, and drunk deeply from the jugs of apple cider. "Where will we stop?" Andrew asked, so tired now he wondered how long he could stay awake in the saddle.

"We'll put up with a friend of my father's," Justin replied, "just a few more miles ahead. He's got a big barn. Our horses will be safe there, and so will we. Then we'll start out early in the morning."

The three hardly remembered turning in to the farm. The Virginians followed Justin to the house, dismounted, and trudged wearily to the door. Justin was welcomed at once by the family, and he and his companions brought in for a late slab of apple pie. Then the kindly farmer led them to the barn, where they stripped the saddles from their horses, rubbed the animals down, fed them and gave them water. Then the boys had climbed wearily to the loft, spread their blankets on the thick hay, and had fallen instantly asleep.

The next morning, the boys were awakened by the farmer's call. "Come and eat," he said. Slowly they rolled out of their blankets and shook the sleep from their eyes.

"I dreamed the whole night!" Andrew said, sitting up.

"I did too." Nathan added.

"So did I," Justin agreed.

"I don't want to think about it!" Justin said decisively. "Let's wash up, and get that breakfast!"

Dreadful scenes of battle — of cannons and muskets firing, of ships' broadsides and clouds of smoke, of falling men, of stumbling wounded, of the fighting retreat from Breed's and Bunker Hills — such scenes had haunted their dreams. None of the boys wanted to talk about these dreams. Quietly they rolled up their blankets, gathered their rifles and packs, and climbed down from the loft. They washed up at the bucket of water beside the kitchen door, and went into the house for breakfast.

A short while later, wide awake now, pleasantly full from a real feast, the three spoke their thanks to the gracious hostess and her husband, and rode away. Each of them had a fat lunch packed in his saddlebags. Each one carried his rifle across the pommel of the saddle, loaded.

"Wonder if the British attacked Cambridge?" Nathan asked as they rode.

"I sure hope not," Andrew replied, "not if the other militia had no more ammunition that the men on the peninsula!"

Then the boys heard a rider approaching at a gallop behind them. Turning in the saddle, they saw a man bent low over his horse's neck, riding for all he was worth. Dust flew from his horse's heels.

"Did the British attack Cambridge?" Justin shouted to the man as he passed.

"No!" the man yelled back. "They retreated to Boston." Then the rider was gone, galloping away as if fleeing from a fire.

"Thank the Lord the British went back!" Andrew said fervently.

"Maybe now our militia will have a chance to get some ammunition before they have to fight again," Nathan said.

And now the three noticed that a terrible weight had been lifted from their minds. The British had retreated to Boston! The American units had been given a reprieve. The long ride that faced them this day no longer seemed so formidable.

The boys kept up a good pace, however. John Turnbull and *The Morning Star* were waiting for them in Newport. From there they'd sail to New York. Justin was as anxious to get to his home as Andrew and Nathan were to get back to theirs. Then the *Morning Star* would take the Virginians home. The three pushed on.

CHAPTER FIFTEEN

WILLIAMSBURG

Sarah and Rachel crossed the street just ahead of a group of marching singing militiamen, then hurried along toward Mrs. Gardiner's house for their violin lesson. The fifes and drums were keeping time for the rousing song of liberty, and the men were singing it lustily and well. Then their captain called out the name of another song.

"Listen, Rachel!" Sarah said excitedly, as the men came abreast of them. "He told them to sing that song about Albion!"

"What's 'Albion' mean?" Rachel asked.

"That's an old name for England, and the words are wonderful! The song is about the Lord's rule over the nations, and His gracious rule through just laws. Listen! It's called 'The New Massachusetts Liberty Song!' " The girls picked up their pace as the men broke into vigorous song.

The seat of science, Albion,
And earth's proud mistress, Rome,
Where now are all their Glories?
We scarce can find their tomb!
Then guard your rights, Americans,
Nor stoop to lawless Sway,

Oppose, Oppose, Oppose it,
For North Americay!

Proud Albion bowed to Caesar,
And numerous lords before,
To Picts, to Danes, to Normans,
And many Masters more;
But we can boast Americans
Have never fall'n a Prey
Huzza! Huzza! Huzza! Huzza!
To North Americay!

   Now the marching company was beside them, the girls were abreast of the middle of the formation, and the full force of the blended voices thrilled their hearts as the men sang in rich harmony:

We led Fair Freedom hither,
And, Lo, the Desert smiled,
A Paradise of Pleasure
New opened in the Wild

Your Harvest, Bold Americans,
No Power shall snatch away!
Preserve! Preserve! Preserve your Rights!
In Free Americay!

Torn from a World of Tyrants,
Beneath this Western Sky
We form'd a New Dominion

A Land of Liberty;
The World shall own we're Freemen here,
And such will ever be!
Huzza! Huzza! Huzza! Huzza!
For Love and Liberty!

Lift up your Hearts, My Heroes!
And swear, with proud Disdain,
The Wretch that would ensnare you,
Shall spread his Net in vain;
Shall Europe empty all her Force,
We'd meet them in Array!
And shout Huzza! Huzza! Huzza!
For brave Americay!

"Oh, that's thrilling!" Sarah exclaimed with tears in her eyes, as the company of men marched past behind their stirring fifes and drums.

The girls hadn't noticed that the marching men with their music had caused them to quicken their own pace! Now, as the company marched away from them, the girls slowed down to their normal walk.

"I'll be so glad when the boys get home!" Rachel said, changing the subject completely, her brown eyes very serious.

"I will, too!" Sarah replied fervently.

The two families had expected Andrew and Nathan to return any day, now; in fact, they'd thought that the *Morning Star* would have returned a week ago. But it had not. And there'd been no word of its coming. But there had been word of a dreadful battle up North between the colonial militia and the British Army.

"What could have happened in Boston, do you think?" Rachel asked.

"I don't know. That messenger just told father that there'd been news that the British had attacked the Patriot militiamen outside the city. A lot of men were killed, mostly British, he said. But he didn't know anything else about it."

"Mother's worried sick about Andrew," Rachel said. "She doesn't say anything. But I can tell. And we pray for them all the time."

"We do, too," Sarah said, her blue eyes clouding. "I know father's surprised that the *Morning Star* isn't back. When mother asks him about it, he tells her that no one can tell when a ship will arrive. 'Everything depends on the winds,' he says. And he reminds her of all the times the boats have arrived days after we've expected them."

"Still, we thought it'd be back a week ago," Rachel said. "Goodness, Sarah, you don't think the boys got caught in that battle around Boston, do you?"

"Of course not!" Sarah said emphatically. "Mother asked Father that, and he told her that the boys are in New York, not Boston, and that those two cities are a long way from each other. Nathan and Andrew couldn't possibly have got caught in the battle!"

The two girls came to the white picket fence that bordered Mrs. Gardiner's house, passed through the gate, and went up the steps to the front door. Every time they came for their lessons, now, they remembered the incident when they'd dropped their music, and had then inadvertently overheard Stephen Bancroft plotting with the messenger.

Before they knocked, Sarah looked at her friend. "I wonder where Stephen is now?" she asked. She had the strangest premonition that they would encounter that young man again.

"I wonder," Rachel answered. "Captain Innes and his men sure gave him a scare. They told him he'd better not even give a hint of sending messages to the Governor, or they'd arrest him for sure!"

"I hope so," Sarah said, blue eyes troubled. "But I'm afraid of him, somehow. I'm sure he hates us, and means to take his revenge on us for reporting him to Captain Innes." She shuddered.

"Well, he's not around here now," Rachel said, "and I don't think we have to worry about him any more." She knocked on the door, and the two girls waited for Mrs. Gardiner to let them in.

The *Morning Star* cut through the choppy waters of Chesapeake Bay, heavily laden with goods taken on board in New York. Andrew and Nathan had parted with Justin Brown and his father, Horatio Brown, and with grateful hearts boarded again their fathers' schooner. Winds had been fair, no danger had threatened from the several British warships they'd seen on the voyage south, and now the boys' hearts lifted as they came closer to home.

The wind was strong, whipping froth from the white caps and blowing this across the surface of the waters, heeling the vessel steeply to the side. Water gushed over the gunwales as the taut sails pressed the sleek vessel through the waves. A crowd of noisy gulls had followed them for the past half hour. Nathan was tossing scraps of food into the wake of the racing vessel, and the birds swooped swiftly after the food, catching it often before it struck the water.

The free Negro, Thomas, was at the wheel, leaning his body into the steering. He'd called John Turnbull a short while before, suggesting they let out the sail to slacken speed and thus reduce the pressure on the boat.

"Not yet, Thomas," Turnbull had said after a swift glance at the sail. "Wait til we pass Yorktown — I want to get out of sight of those British ships before we slow her down." He returned to the bow and continued coiling a stiff new line.

But the strain on the mast and rigging had increased suddenly as the wind itself had grown stronger. Turnbull ran back from the bow and took the wheel.

"Let 'er out a bit," he called.

"Yes, sir," Thomas said, relieved — he'd been worrying about the terrific pressure on the the mast and rigging. Thomas called the boys, and soon the three had loosened the lines and let out the sails.

Immediately the *Morning Star* slowed its pace. The waves ceased to smash over the vessel's side, and the rough pitching was lessened.

"Thomas," Turnbull called. "You were right! That wind was stronger than I realized!"

"You were at the bow, Cap'n," Thomas said. "You couldn't feel the wheel as I could!"

Andrew and Nathan joined Turnbull at the wheel as Thomas went forward to continue coiling the line that Turnbull had left.

"There's a lesson here, boys," Turnbull said. "Thomas could feel the pressure on the wheel. He knew that a sudden increase in the wind could put us over in a jiffy — and wreck the boat!" He paused, and looked over at the shore reflectively. "You know, it's best to have some reserve — in everything in life, in fact — and not push things to the limit just for a temporary advantage."

Now the schooner sailed more easily, more smoothly, cutting through the blue waters with a white bow of foam and spray.

"Look at all the shipping!" Andrew exclaimed, pointing to the number of sails in the great bay.

"No signs of a British blockade here!" Nathan replied.

"Not yet, at any rate," Andrew answered. "But from what happened around Boston last week, there's no telling what the British will do next."

"I think they're still hoping to keep the colonies divided," John Turnbull said thoughtfully, as he held the wheel in an iron grip. "After all, it was Massachusetts militia that fought their troops in Boston. Not all the colonies were involved."

"Not entirely Massachusetts men, Sir," Andrew answered. "There were Connecticut militia too, and John Stark's New Hampshire riflemen."

"Good point," Turnbull replied. "Still, they're all northern Colonies — Virginia had no part in it."

"Is that why no British ship has tried to stop us?" Nathan asked.

"I don't think so," Turnbull answered. "Remember, it takes a while for news to travel down the seacoast. The ships we've passed probably have no idea what's happened — they sure don't know as much about that battle as you two! And, as I said, the British Government has no policy directed against the Middle and Southern Colonies yet. I say — not 'yet.' "

"Then you think that they will soon?" Andrew asked.

"Depends," Turnbull said. "It all depends on what Virginia and the other colonies decide to do. That's why they've sent their delegates to the Continental Congress in Philadelphia — to decide what to do. But until the other colonies take action against the British, I don't think Parliament will order any action against them."

"But that was war around Breed's and Bunker Hill!" Nathan said. "The Americans shot a thousand British troops!"

"That was real war," the Master agreed. He leaned his powerful body against the wheel, took his tobacco pouch from his pocket, and began to pack his pipe. "But it was a Massachusetts war — plus some men from New Hampshire and Connecticut, as you say. And that still leaves the Middle and Southern Colonies out of the fighting."

"But if the Congress decides to take up the cause of Massachusetts," Andrew said, "then the British will fight us all."

"You're right," Turnbull agreed. "If the Congress decides to make Massachusetts' cause their own, then Parliament will have no reason to spare the other colonies. Remember, Parliament's declared that they have total power and authority over all the colonies in everything — that means, there's no constitutional, no legal, no legislative protection from any decision the English Government adopts."

"But that's more power than the King has over England!" Andrew exclaimed. "Since the Magna Carta, the King himself has been bound by law and by constitution. He can't break those!"

"He can now. You see, Parliament put itself over the English constitution and all other legal restraints. They made themselves supreme when they deposed the former king and called William of Orange to take the English throne. Now they have absolute, total power over everyone in England. The King is said to be the sovereign 'in Parliament', that is, through Parliament. But since King George's bought the votes of so many of Parliament's members — with money, and titles, and government favors and jobs — he can get them to do anything he wants. So, actually, Parliament's doing his bidding when it claims total authority and power over the colonies."

"Then we have no legal protection for our churches either?" Andrew exclaimed.

"None at all," Turnbull said. "Parliament — or, the King acting through Parliament — can close all the Protestant churches, and order us all to be members of the Church of England if they want to. In fact, that's exactly what the English Bishops in the House of Lords want them to do. And that's what a lot of folks fear that they will do — just like they made Roman Catholicism the official religion in the Province of Canada."

A flock of gulls flew close just then, coming from behind Andrew and Nathan, and crying out loudly as they passed over. The two boys ducked suddenly, and Turnbull laughed at their startled faces. Then he continued.

"Most people in Virginia, of course, are members of the Church of England, but not all. Some are Presbyterians, like your folks, and there's a bunch of Baptists. But in the Northern Colonies, and the Middle Colonies, things are different. Those people's forefathers fled England to escape the Church of England because they thought that the Church of England hadn't been reformed enough at the time of the Reformation. So those folks are scared to death that Parliament will declare their churches illegal, jail their preachers, and tax them to support the Church of England — and make them become members of that Church and fine them if they won't come to their worship."

Turnbull puffed on his pipe as he reflected on the religious situation in the British Province of Canada. "Boys, when Parliament made Roman Catholicism the official religion of Canada it terrified the Protestant Colonies of New England and New York! Too many people from those colonies lost family members in the fires and dungeons of the Roman Inquisition. They can't be happy with Catholicism being made the required religion in the British Province just north of them! That's what they know could happen here, too, because Parliament has all power, all authority, with nothing to stop them at all."

"That's scary!" Nathan said, shocked.

"It is indeed," Turnbull agreed. "That's why the men in Massachusetts and New Hampshire and Connecticut have been getting ready to defend themselves against the British raids. And that's why they were able to fight back when the British troops shot their militiamen in Lexington."

Later that afternoon, the *Morning Star* swept into College Landing near Williamsburg, and docked. Two wagons were there, their barrels of goods standing beside them, waiting to be loaded on the next schooner. Andrew and Nathan got their packs and rifles from the cabin below, bade farewell to John Turnbull, and rode in the first wagon that headed back to Williamsburg. Thomas rode with them, eager to see his family.

"See you in town, boys," John Turnbull called, as they rode off. "Tell your fathers to send the wagons for their goods tomorrow. Tell them they made a lot of money on this trip! That won't make them unhappy!"

"And Thomas," the skipper called, "tell Mary I've got some cloth for her, and dolls for the girls. But don't tell your son about the knife. I want to surprise him with that!"

"Yes, sir," Thomas called back, his black face grinning broadly. "You be sure to call me back here if you need me."

"Don't worry," Turnbull said. "I will — but not for three days." He waved, and turned back to the sloop.

The afternoon sun was sinking behind the trees when the wagon stopped in front of the Edwards' home. Andrew and Nathan jumped down, retrieved their packs and rifles, thanked the driver, and trudged toward Nathan's house first.

"Seems like we've been gone a year!" Andrew said wearily, as they mounted the steps. Lights shone with a cheerful glow from the windows, however, and this picked up the boys' spirits.

"At least a year!" Nathan agreed. "Maybe three!" He knocked, then opened the door and entered the house. Andrew, just behind him, heard a scream from inside. Then, through the open door, he saw Nathan's sister Sarah rush toward her brother and throw herself into his arms. Nathan dropped his pack to the floor and hugged her back.

Mrs. Edwards hurried into the hall then. "Nathan!" she cried, and rushed toward her son. Sarah stepped back so that her mother could give her son a hug.

Andrew came through the door, and stopped. When Sarah stepped back from Nathan, she saw Andrew for the first time. Her blue eyes grew wide and she stood still for a brief moment, staring at him. Then she cried "Andrew!" Rushing toward him she threw her arms around his neck and burst into tears, her face against his chest.

Startled, Andrew dropped his pack to the floor. Gripping his long rifle in one hand, he put his other arm around the girl and held her awkwardly. She'd never done this before, and he didn't know what to do.

Mr. Edwards came into the room then, glanced quickly at Andrew's red face, winked at the boy with a big grin, then gripped Nathan's hand and pounded his shoulder. "Welcome home, Son!" he said.

Andrew's face was crimson now, and he didn't know what to say — so he didn't say anything. He just stood still, his strong arm holding the girl around her waist as she cried with joy on his chest. At least he hoped it was joy. He guessed it was. But you never could tell about girls, he'd found. Sometimes you just couldn't figure 'em out.

CHAPTER SIXTEEN

THE DARK CLOUDS OF WAR

"It's inevitable, now," Edmund Pendleton said, gazing gravely at the group of men seated around the table in the Raleigh Tavern.

"After I left the Congress to return to Williamsburg, the delegates there chose Colonel George Washington to lead the Continental Army that was camped around Boston."

"That was a fine choice," William Hendricks said.

"A fine choice indeed," George Wythe agreed. A dignified man, Wythe was Professor of Law at the College of William and Mary. He was one of the leading legal authorities in Virginia, and had long been a firm defender of the historic rights and liberties of the American Colonies.

"But not an uncontested choice," Pendleton added. A large portly man, of immense dignity and parliamentary skill, he had been elected President of the Continental Congress which met in Philadelphia. He'd only left that Congress to return to Williamsburg and resume his leadership of the Virginia House of Burgesses after the British Governor had fled to a warship off Norfolk.

"There were various factors that determined their choice of Colonel Washington," Pendleton continued. "Many of the New Englanders really wanted one of their own military men to command the army outside Boston. They argued that there were a number of men with far greater experience than Colonel Washington who could better lead the New England militia forces."

"Why then was Washington chosen?" William Hendricks asked.

"John and Sam Adams knew that Virginia was the key to Colonial unity and success," Pendleton replied, shifting in his chair.

"They thought the choice of a Virginian to lead the colonial armies would be a strong point in stressing the union of the colonies in their resistance to British tyranny. They know that New England alone cannot wage war successfully with Great Britain. And Colonel Washington had great respect among the men there as an experienced Indian fighter. They knew he'd been head of the Virginia militia, and that he was also very familiar with British military thinking and tactics."

"They're quite correct in that," George Wythe agreed. "Colonel Washington served with great gallantry under the unfortunate General Braddock, and actually was responsible for rescuing hundreds of demoralized British soldiers from that dreadful defeat, and leading their successful retreat."

"Had Braddock and the other English officers listened to him," Edmund Pendleton said, "and let their troops fight behind trees like the Frenchmen and the Indians who had ambushed them, they might not have panicked, and fewer of them would have been shot down. As it was, the soldiers were forced to stand in their closed ranks and fight in the open. This made them perfect targets for the Frenchmen and Indians who shot from behind trees. They never had a chance."

"Washington's a remarkable leader," George Wythe said reflectively. "He's a magnificent horseman, a superior fighting man of immense strength and character, and he possesses the gift of leading men."

"And he has great dignity," Pendleton added. "Well, we must pray, gentlemen, that he will quickly develop those qualities of moving large bodies of men in the face of the British professional army. For King George and Parliament are most certainly determined that the colonies will not be freed from their absolute tyranny, and are hiring thousands of experienced soldiers from the Germanic States to serve with their own regiments. Washington will have a formidable task!"

A man rushed into the dark-paneled room then, and handed Edmund Pendleton a folded paper. Pendleton took this, thanked the man, untied the string that held the paper closed, and read the letter. His face became grave.

"Governor Dunmore has been reinforced by some soldiers from the British garrison in Florida," he said tersely. "He's quartering these men in Norfolk. And he's got several vessels with him now. Our informants tell us that he means to attack our plantations and supply depots as soon as he has enough men."

"Are his ships moving upriver toward us?" William Hendricks asked quickly.

"This note does not say so, William," Pendleton replied. "But of course it is always possible. Are your schooners in the river now?

"One of them is," Hendricks said. He rose. "If you will excuse me, Gentlemen, I'll ride to the landing and warn John Turnbull."

Shortly afterwards, William Hendricks and Andrew stood on the deck of the *Morning Star*, deep in conversation with John Turnbull.

"Don't worry, William," Turnbull said calmly, as he puffed on his white pipe. "We sail with great care — I never go out of the river without first locating the warships. And I always take the most shallow course where those larger vessels cannot follow me. I'm more worried about logs in the water than I am about those British ships."

"Well, there's no sign of war against us here in Virginia as yet," Hendricks said. "When it comes, it could come without warning, of course. The first who'd know would be those on the ships the British captured! But, for now at least, we seem safe. I just wanted to warn you of Governor Dunmore's activity. He's gathering a group of small ships with which to harass our coasts."

As William Hendricks and Andrew rode back to Williamsburg from the landing, they discussed the further ominous news that William had heard from Edmund Pendleton in the Raleigh Tavern that morning. "The most immediate danger we face," he told Andrew, "is from the west. Governor Dunmore sent his agent, Dr. John Connolly, to meet with Indian chiefs on on western borders. Dunmore's aim is to buy the allegiance of those tribes, and finance their war against our western settlements."

"But that's terrible!" Andrew replied, shocked. "That's what the French have been doing for a hundred years! How could an Englishman pay the Indians to wage their kind of war against farmers in the western settlements? He knows how they torture and burn their victims! And what they do to women and girls!"

"He does indeed know this," William Hendricks agreed. "He knows exactly how the Indian tribes fight men and women and children — he's told us this many times when he's asked the House of Burgesses to raise money for his wars against the warring and burning tribes. But, remember, he's serving a tyrannical government in London. Such a government has no hesitation in turning any kind of force against citizens who do not submit."

"Things do not look good, Father," Andrew said.

"They do not," his father agreed. "Yet, it is these dreadful circumstances that have caused many of our people to realize that if we're going to preserve our society, our lives and freedoms and religion, we must be prepared to defend them. Only now, we defend them not against the French and the Indians, but against our own government! But we're not at war yet — not here in the South! So I'm sending you with John Turnbull to Bermuda. The *Morning Star's* almost loaded. You'll take a full cargo, and bring back military supplies: gunpowder, muskets, flints, in addition to other goods. We've got to procure as much of these as we can, before the British warships try to stop us."

That evening, Andrew sat in the Edwards' kitchen, eating a thick piece of pie Sarah had handed him.

"How does your father know that it's safe for you to sail to the Caribbean?" she asked, her eyes clouded with worry at the prospect of Andrew sailing into waters where British warships might be encountered.

"Well, we're a small ship," he explained. "And the *Morning Star* is fast. And we'll probably not see a British warship anyway. Virginia's vessels haven't yet been attacked by their ships. We'll be back before the situation gets dangerous, Father says. The British may be planning war against us, but they haven't declared it yet, and they haven't started to fight us."

"But the Governor was outraged that his Palace in Williamsburg was broken into three times, and all the muskets and pistols and swords were stolen!" Sarah replied. "Isn't that an act of war?"

"Well, it sure seems like it!" Andrew agreed with a grin. He told her of the group of militiamen that had almost captured Governor Dunmore when the Governor had been so foolish as to visit his plantation on the river.

"Still, that was just a bunch of young men that robbed the Palace. Our leaders said they had nothing to do with it. And the men who almost captured the Governor were not acting under orders from our leaders in Williamsburg. So nothing official's happened yet to cause us to fear any danger."

"But, Andrew," she insisted, "the British could declare war at any time they choose! Then it'll be too late to protest — you know they won't listen!"

Mr. Edwards came into the room then, and Andrew was relieved that he didn't have to answer Sarah's questions. "Nathan's going to Winchester with the wagons, Andrew," Nelson Edwards said. "Think you and John Turnbull and Thomas can handle this voyage without him?" He had a twinkle in his eye.

"We'll try, sir," Andrew replied with a grin. "I'd sure rather be sailing smooth seas in the *Morning Star* than riding a wagon and horses to Winchester!"

"So would he!" Nelson Edwards laughed. "But I need him to make this trip for us, while you go to Bermuda. Just keep your eyes open, and get back in a hurry." He shook Andrew's hand, then walked out of the room.

"When do you sail?" Sarah asked him.

"Tomorrow morning," he replied. "I wanted to say that this is great pie, but I didn't want to call your father's attention to the fact that you'd given me the first piece."

"Oh, he knows that!" she laughed. "He looked at the pie when he came in the room." She laughed as she went to the cupboard and cut him another thick piece.

"Sometimes I think he's half serious when he says he'll beat me for eating from his pies before he gets to taste them!" Andrew said with a grin.

"Oh, he knows I'll bake him more. He's just teasing you."

Andrew walked home thoughtfully. He knew that his father wouldn't send him on the *Morning Star* if he thought that the seas were dangerous for Virginian vessels. That night, his father led them all in prayer. He prayed specifically for the safety of the *Morning Star*, and for Thomas, and Turnbull, and Andrew.

Far across the Atlantic Ocean, leading members of the Parliamentary committees responsible for British naval and military affairs worked late in their offices. They were planning for war — war against their American Colonies. The mighty power of the British Empire was about to be re-deployed. Administrators dictated letters to secretaries, secretaries made copies, and messengers took the copies to the heads of the naval and military departments. Slowly, inexorably, the mighty power of Great Britain would be withdrawn from the far corners of the globe; ships and regiments of soldiers would head for England, where they'd be re-directed — to North America. There they would be joined ultimately by thirty thousand professional soldiers hired from various Germanic States in Europe. England did not intend to allow her richest and most profitable colonies to escape her rule! She wanted their resources — and their money!

That same evening, on the hills outside Boston, a big blue-clad officer mounted on a great white horse held a telescope in his hands as he studied the British forts below. Mounted officers of his staff sat on their horses on either side. Behind them stretched the camp fires of militia regiments from various American colonies. The Americans had bottled up the British troops in Boston, and did not intend to allow the redcoats to make another destructive raid on the towns and farms outside the city as they had on Lexington and Concord. Finally the big Virginian snapped shut his telescope, and turned to his second in command. "We must drive them out of Boston!"

Wheeling his mount, the magnificent horseman headed at a gallop back down the hill, his long cape billowing behind him as he rode. General Washington's staff wheeled their mounts as well, and followed him as quickly as they could. As the men rode toward the American lines, they heard in the distance the ominous beat of military drums.

They were the drums of war.

THE THIRTEEN COLONIES
1763 - 1775

Great Britain's King had broken Faith, his solemn Covenant,
And – Drunk with Power – planned to end the Liberties
God sent
To this Fair Land, these Colonies, who'd known God's holy
Word
As Guide to each State's Government, as Pledge that He
was Lord;

That every Earthly Potentate was under His Command,
And none could wield Authority but by His Will and Hand.
King George defied this Lord, and threw off England's own
Constraints,
And sent his Armies to subdue the Folk whose firm Com-
plaints

Had pleaded for the Justice their own Charters granted
them–
To no avail! King George just ordered Ships and Guns and
Men
To master these Free Colonies, to Tax them at his Will,
Restrict their own Religion, and with Bandits then to fill

The Offices that governed them, the Posts and Magistrates:
Rewards for his own Favorites who cared not for the Fate
Of Colonies whose Laws they bent, of Citizens they
wronged,
Of People who sought only Peace and desperately longed

For Order and Stability, for Justice and for Law;
But saw their Liberties instead devoured within the Maw
Of ever-lasting Government, with one Titanic Head,
Whose Officers broke all Restraint and who no longer had

Strict Bounds to their Authority, firm Hedges to their Power,
True Limits to their Force, to stop their endless Drive to
  Tower
Above all Local Government, all Customs, Laws, and Rule,
And reign – as Gods unchecked by Law! But Colonists
  weren't Fools.

For they had learned from Scripture that th' Eternal
  Heaven's King
Had set strict Bounds to Earthly Rule, and would most
  surely bring
Dread Tyranny and Slavery to Men who spurned His Sway,
Who let their Earthly Caesars grow unchecked from Day to
  Day.

So brave Men stood – with Guns in Hand – and faced the
  Tyrant's Power;
They owned that God had set His King on Zion's Holy
  Tower.
They prayed – and fought – their Land to save from God-
  less Government;
They marched with General Washington to free this Conti-
  nent.

Acknowledgements

Quote on pp. 128-129 from Willard M. Wallace, *Appeal to Arms*, Chicago: Quandrangle Books, 1951, pp. 41-42.

Quote on p. 131 from *Appeal to Arms*, p. 43.